AMAZING WOMAN
DIVINE
LEGACY

THE RADIANT RESET

Claim a New Narrative of Sacred Confidence
Rise in Your Spiritual Purpose

Marsh Engle

Debra Shoults Bettendorf, Candice Smith Güzelışık,
Priscilla Hataway, Ella Nebeker, Becky Norwood,
Kristi Lynn Olson, CeCe Sanchez and Diane Sova

Along with additional Mentors, Entrepreneurs and Changemakers

©2025 Marsh Engle
The Radiant Reset
Claim a New Narrative of Sacred Confidence – Rise in Your Spiritual Purpose

Amazing Woman Divine Legacy
Join the millions of women who are rising in the wealth of their spiritual purpose, reshaping their sacred work, and serving the world.

eBook ISBN: 978-1-965761-34-2
Paperback ISBN: 978-1-965761-35-9
Hardcover ISBN: 978-1-965761-36-6
Ingram Spark ISBN: 978-1-965761-37-3
Library of Congress Control Number: 2025903797

Cover Design by Marsh Engle
Interior Design by Marigold2k
Published by Spotlight Publishing House –
https: SpotlightPublishingHouse.com

All rights reserved. Printed in the United States of America. No part of this book may be used or reproduced in any written form or by electronic or mechanical means, including information storage and retrieval systems, without written permission from the author, except for the use of brief quotations in a book review.

For More Information about
Amazing Woman Nation go to:
www.AmazingWomanNation.com

AMAZING WOMAN
DIVINE
LEGACY
THE RADIANT RESET

Claim a New Narrative of Sacred Confidence
Rise in Your Spiritual Purpose

Marsh Engle

Debra Shoults Bettendorf, Candice Smith Güzelışık,
Priscilla Hataway, Ella Nebeker, Becky Norwood,
Kristi Lynn Olson, CeCe Sanchez and Diane Sova

Goodyear, Arizona

Table of Contents

Dedication ix
Preface xi
Significance of the Peacock xv
Introduction xxi

Featured Authors:

From Limitation to Radiance:
Expanding Through Presence 1
   —Priscilla Hataway 1
Whispers from the Past: Wisdom for the Future 33
   —Diane Sova 33
Finding the Feminine Face of God 67
   —Kristi Lynn Olson 67
Awaken the Artistry of Alchemy 97
   —CeCe Sanchez 97
Does Your Soul Shine? 131
   —Becky Norwood 131
The Most Important Relationship You'll Ever Have 163
   —Debra Shoults Bettendorf 163
Divine Potential
Lessons From Women Past & Present 195
   —Candice Smith Güzelişik 195
Finding Stillness Through Self-Love:
A Most Radiant Quality of Your Divine Nature 229
   —Ella Nebeker 229

Radiant Insights:

Rocio Ortiz Luevano 253
Niloo Golshan 260
Carol Patricia Koppelman 270
Conni Ponturo 274

Claim Your Sacred Confidence. 282
Write a Radiant Reset Statement 282
About Amazing Woman Nation 294
Acknowledgments 297
About Marsh Engle 299
Amazing Woman Books by Marsh Engle 302

*There comes a time when every woman is called
to stand in the power of her sacred confidence —
to claim a narrative steeped in her worth and
rooted in a rich understanding of
her connection to a greater purpose —
acknowledging the wealth of her unique gifts
and trusting herself to harness them to
make a difference in her life,
her community and, ultimately, in the world.*

That time is now.

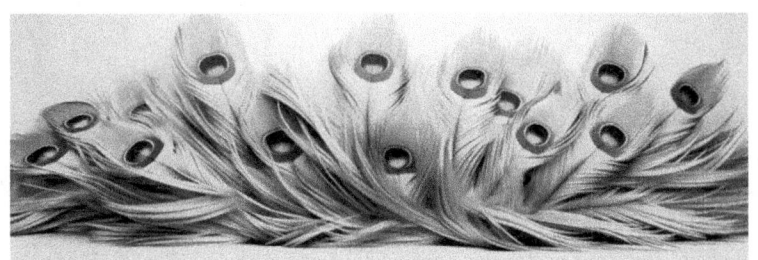

Dedication

Amazing Woman, every time we remind the woman next to us that her voice is the vessel of her giftedness… something takes place… a radiance of respect is ignited within her and within you… because what we acknowledge in another fuels the flame of the same within ourselves… and that's how we bring about a radiant reset… that's how a new realm of sacred confidence emerges.

That's how we live our Divine Legacy.

Amazing Woman, this book is dedicated to you and the reflection of love you bring to life.

There's a rumbling happening in the hearts of
women… it's the calling of our next evolution…
a call to give voice to our sacred confidence…
to rise in our purpose.
And own a new narrative for our future.

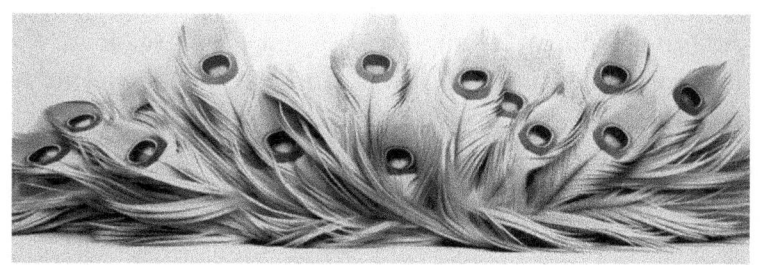

Preface

Written by Marsh Engle

*There's a rumbling happening in the hearts
of women… it's the calling of
our next evolution… a call to give voice
to our sacred confidence…
to rise in our purpose. And own a new
narrative for our future.*

There comes a time when every woman is called to rise in the power of her spiritual purpose and embrace a rich understanding of her connection to a greater calling — acknowledging the wealth of her unique gifts and her ability to harness them to make a difference in her life, her communities and, ultimately, in the world. *Amazing Woman, that time is now.*

**Together we'll ignite a RADIANT RESET and
break free from the invisible barriers that unconsciously
stop us from making the bold moves to serve the
world in ways needed now.**

Amazing Woman, it's time to step out of the shadows, the fatigue of silencing our voices, and the kind of relentless pursuit that's driven by societal expectations — these are the constraints that all too often sabotage the energetic force within us and steal the sacred confidence to challenge status quo, step into centerstage, and act upon our highest creative callings.

This is our call to finally and forever release agreements that cause us to edit our truth, silence our voices, limit the vision for our future, and hide the radiance of our true self.

Through the pages of THE RADIANT RESET, you'll discover how women are rapidly dismantling outdated narratives, amplifying their voices and serving in the ways the world needs most today. Their words are authentic. And their insights revealing. What's more is that their vulnerability offers an intimate window into the potency of their own RADIANT RESET journey — guiding us into the kind of sacred confidence that will shape how we intuit, create, think, and work as a woman.

Your next evolution is calling to you now!

Certainly, there are periods in our lives when we feel overwhelmed by circumstances or events — moments when we feel lost or disconnected and discouraged. However, being harsh on ourselves during such times distances us from our true spiritual power and limits our ability to foster a confident relationship with our broader potential.

These moments, though they may seem like we've lost our direction, are in fact opportunities for the growth and evolution of our spiritual purpose. As we experience significant changes in our lives and the world around us, it is essential to recognize and embrace new abilities, insights, and directions as they present themselves — navigating our spiritual path and rising into a vivid vision of our future.

When a woman rises in her spiritual purpose and claims a new narrative of sacred confidence, everything changes!

Practical exercises, journal writing prompts, and affirmative quotes interweave with intimate personal stories and potent transformative teachings offered by a dynamic collective of spiritual entrepreneurs, trailblazing coaches, creative mentors, and more — providing you with a guidebook to create a RADIANT RESET of your own — a new narrative that carries with it the potential to reshape the next evolution of your work, your relationships, and ultimately the world around you.

A new era of spiritual purpose is here and it's unleashing a radiant power to forge a fresh narrative for our future, one rooted in sacred confidence.

Finally, THE RADIANT RESET illuminates your path forward. As you journey into the creation of your own radiant reset, I invite you to hold close the truth of your heart, the voice of your spiritual purpose — and remember the unwavering strength of your sacred confidence.

This book will show you how.

Marsh Engle

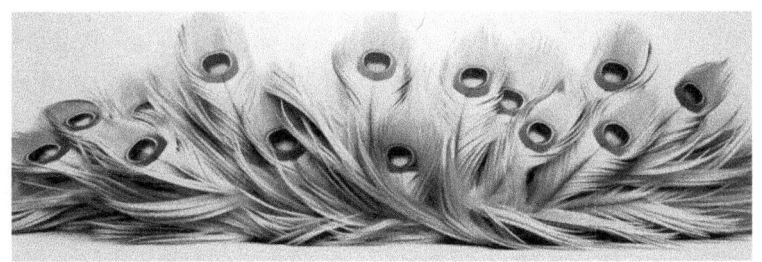

Significance of the Peacock

*A sacred symbol of elegance, beauty,
spiritual awakening, wealth, and the divine feminine.*

Sacred Meanings Associated with the Peacock

1. Beauty and Self-expression: The radiant display of the peacock's feathers represents beauty while its colorful display symbolizes self-expression.

2. Creativity and Life: The peacock feathers are often associated with the beauty of life, a passionate display of creativity and celebration.

3. Potent Energy: Peacocks are powerful creatures with potent energy and that, of course, includes their feathers.

4. New Beginnings and Potentials: The Peacock reminds of the power of being present to positive and new opportunities.

5. Spiritual Awakening: Possibly the most significant of all, the peacock is recognized as a symbol of transformation, renewal, and progress.

A new era of spiritual purpose is here and it's unleashing a radiant power to forge a fresh narrative for our future, one rooted in sacred confidence.

We Are Remembering

We are the ones remembering our spiritual purpose blazing a new trail paved in our intuitive intelligence, feminine strengths, and hearts of wisdom.

*We are the ones remembering —
the ones linking arms to rise together —
the ones answering the call to serve.*

We are the ones.

*We are the ones remembering the potency of our voices.
And awakening a consciousness of feminine esteem —
transforming the landscape of leadership.*

*We are the ones who stay true to our spiritual purpose,
the ones anchoring in a new dimension of
sacred confidence and claiming our place as the
amazing women we are meant to be.*

We are the ones.

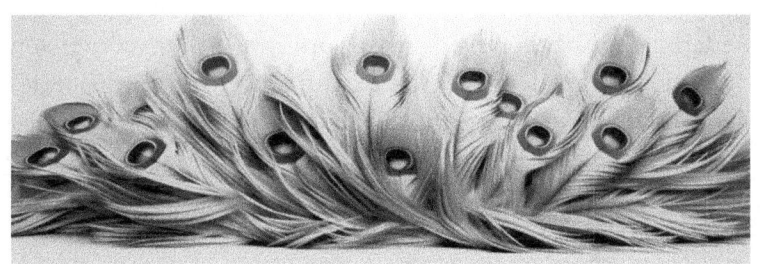

Introduction

> *For years I held the image in my heart*
> *of this picture of what it would be like to walk in the footsteps*
> *of the Divine Feminine.*
> *That's what brought me to this sacred place,*
> *one of the most holy regions in the world.*
> *What I did not know is how every step would*
> *transform the way I define my future.*

I've got my iPhone, my cross-body bag and my water bottle strung around my neck; my hiking boots precisely laced making certain they are especially tight around my ankles. Across my face is a combination of hesitancy, sheer enthusiasm, and the tiniest hint of self-doubt. My heart is certain that I am where I want to be, or, unquestionably where I *need* to be. This is what it looks and feels like to follow one's heart, even when, especially when it may not make solid sense.

I can still remember the strength of my younger body. That's before a series of random, significant and very scary injuries redefined my full range of motion and, if I'm completely honest, uprooted my sense of confidence. Along the way I let fear seep deep into my bones creating a distance and a disconnect between my sense of safety in the world and the expression of my soul.

But now I'm here. And the path is even more rugged than I anticipated. My enduring *'let no one see your doubt'* stoic-self kicked in. I told myself I would power-through, make myself be brave. Even though I quietly wondered why no one had spoken about the intensity of the multi-mile daily hikes, collection of steep steps, rugged climbs along the side of mountains and days of transversing the hidden trails that spread across France.

Maybe I knew the journey would be exceptionally challenging.

Maybe people had offered up their concerns and caution.

Truthfully, the desire for this journey was rooted so deeply in my heart that it's unlikely anything or anyone could have discouraged me. In other words, if someone had voiced their thoughts about the adventure I was embarking on, I would have surely turned down the volume of their concerns.

For years I held the image in my heart of this picture of what it would be like to walk in the footsteps of the Divine Feminine. That's what brought me to this place. It was my idea. It was my decision. For as long as I can remember, I'd immersed myself in the study of feminine leadership —

beginning in a time when feminine leadership was only seen as a foreign 'concept' — making no sense to too many. And now, this journey would lead me to set foot on the very land — the hallowed ground — where countless others who celebrated the infinite powers of the Divine Feminine had walked before me.

I wondered: *Why have I brought myself here now?*

Maybe I wanted to be reacquainted with the me that once lived bold, risk-taking and courageous. Maybe I wanted to remember how once upon a time this kind of confidence moved through me from the inside out… and showed up as a brilliant light streaming from my eyes and originating from my heart… a kind of spirit that I can only call sacred confidence… maybe I longed to remember a time when I was in my wholeness… I was undivided.

I was drawn to this sacred place, more of a calling to reawaken than a desire to travel. I wanted to remember. And collect those parts of me that were missing in action… the innate qualities of my spiritual gifts that had gone unacknowledged and hidden away deep in the crevasses of my unexpressed potentials.

This journey through the sacred cathedrals and forests was a chance to immerse myself in the palpable energies of one of the most holy regions of the world, layered in a plethora of unspoken truths. This was it. It was my opportunity to nudge loose and release the tight grip that held so closely onto an antiquated self-image.

I questioned what 'need' was anchoring this image in place. And even more, what lay beneath the image that was now declaring itself ready to be seen and heard?

I was walking a sacred journey that was taking me into a world deeply steeped in history and beauty — not only known for its stunning landscapes but also for its spiritual significance, particularly in celebrating the feminine aspects of divinity.

I immediately felt myself drawn into a reflection and a remembrance of times past.

This was a journey into an era and a place where history reveals the feminine voice was severely suppressed. I started to feel and sense the anguish from a period when the feminine was disregarded — a time when our abilities, healing powers, intuition, and love were driven into obscurity, concealed from view. More tragically, how the women who preceded us faced punishment or death simply for embodying spiritual, insightful, intelligent, feminine leadership, serving as celebrants of the Divine.

Year upon year we've endured a multitude of labels. We've been erased from history, our contributions ignored. We've been criticized for being too much — too bold, too intelligent, too outspoken, and even for being too feminine.

As I wandered along the trails and engulfed myself in the landscape, I began to consider the enduring influence of this legacy on women today. These reflections sparked a cascade of inquiries within me.

With each question, I plunged deeper and further, absorbing everything I could about how we've been conditioned to resist our power.

Is our reluctance to speak our truths and give words to our wisdom in some way rooted in the silencing of those who came before us?
Are we subjecting ourselves to self-imposed penalties because of the severe punishments they endured?
Do our bodies cling to feelings of shame due to the humiliation experienced by previous generations?
Are we still dwelling in the shadows of history, and if so, what steps must we take to create a new narrative for our future?

For more than twenty years, I have been ardently committed to amplifying women's voices — a sacred call to honor the divine feminine within each woman — cultivating an environment rich in collaboration, self-recognition and purpose-driven achievement. In essence, creating a sacred environment where women felt seen and heard — an environment designed to shift the culture of our leadership and success.

Throughout the years, there have been plenty of occasions when I faced fear head-on and pushed through regardless.

And there have also been times when I have consciously or unconsciously restrained myself. I've undervalued my worth, felt insignificant, and yearned to truly acknowledge and honor my role in the world.

There have also been periods when I was unwavering in my drive to fulfill my calling to serve, convincing myself that I was fearless in my endeavors, yet never truly permitting myself to be fully expressed — to be seen or be heard. And now I'm here deep in the forest on a mountainside immersed in the memories of a time when the true beauty, insights, and power of women was harshly denied. And I am remembering.

Yet, I carry onward. I am putting my feet on the ground. As rugged as trail before me appears, I am devoted to moving forward. This commitment is driven by a rumbling in my heart that tells me I'm here for a purpose — and with each step that purpose is becoming more and more clear.

I'm here to allow myself to see with new eyes.

So, I ask:

How am I denying my most radiant expression
— my wholeness —
the feminine aspects of divinity?

Asking this question opened the flood gates to an outpouring of realizations. A new perspective began to reveal itself. With each revelation, a transformation within me began to unfold.

A new consciousness was awakening.
Aspects that had been long denied were now
rising in my awareness, compelling me to dig deeper.
A flood of unacknowledged truths was guiding me into
a new way of seeing and defining who I truly am.

With this stream of awareness came the image of a magical thread woven into the tapestry of womankind — a legacy of sacred confidence — the wealth of our feminine aspects of divinity fully embraced and celebrated — a revelation of untapped potentials — an expansive expression of creativity, intuitive intelligence, healing abilities, innate wisdom, and boundless respect.

The more I let go — the more I surrendered into what I can only call a *'tread of remembering'* — and I found myself immersed in a stream of awakening.

Do you see who you truly are?

Do you remember your healing?

Do you remember your calling?

Do you remember your sacred confidence?

As the stream of awakenings continued to unfold, it gently dismantled the layers of distorted self-judgment and the masks of 'less than' beliefs and limitations that had been worn for lifetimes. As the dismantling persisted, an expansive recognition and appreciation of my Divine Self was unveiled, allowing long-suppressed inner truths to be called back and transmuted into strength, power and wisdom.

Marsh Engle

The awakening of feminine esteem
opens our eyes to a new level of consciousness —
a sacred confidence that is more than just a shift
in perception but a radiant metamorphosis
that touches every facet of our being.

I sensed within the depths of my being that a new domain of luminous feminine esteem was emerging, unleashing a dynamic and more profound state of consciousness — a consciousness essential for women to forge a fresh narrative for their future, one rooted in sacred confidence.

The questions I posed were evolving, gaining a fresh perspective — the answers I sought were no longer rooted in a desire to spark an internal transformation. Instead, the internal shift that had already occurred was now prompting me to ask questions that would manifest an outward expression.

Am I hindering my forward movement?

How can I invest the reservoir of my untapped potential?

That's when Joan of Arc's words resonated deeply within my heart, echoing with clarity and strength.

> *"I am not afraid. I was born to do this."*

I stopped in my tracks and repeated the words aloud:

> *"I am not afraid. I was born to do this."*

Each word was imbued with profound insight, vibrant energy, sheer courage, and vast significance.

Each word affirmed we are equipped with the capability to confront and even transform the most difficult situations.

Each word conveyed our capacity to set aside procrastination, navigate setbacks, and trust in the power of timing.

The words stirred me. I was remembering.

We can transcend overthinking, excessive questioning, and discouragement offered by others — including what has become societal norms, influences and limitations.

But I sensed the words were saying even more.

They were urging me to delve even deeper.

Slowly, I spoke the sentence again. This time pausing at every word allowing its essence to land in my heart and breath power into my consciousness…

"I am not afraid. I was born to do this."

That's when the RADIANT RESET clicked in…

> *In this moment, I was enveloped in feminine esteem and a sacred confidence that reminded me it was safe for me to let go of past attachments and allow myself to fully embrace self-trust.*

Marsh Engle

I let go of the identity that kept me striving to live into a definition that was never my own.

I now understood what it means to stay true to the path of MY spiritual purpose.

As you take steps to move forward to embody the essence of your spiritual purpose — to create your own Radiant Reset — begin by claiming a new narrative for yourself, one that encourages, collaborates, praises, values, and respects the woman you are and the woman you are becoming — one who celebrates, honors, and expresses her gifts, abilities, insights, and ideas.

Let yourself see with new eyes.

Hold nothing back.

Take up space.

Stretch the edges of what's been done before.

Let this be an invitation to rewrite your future — this time, write it as a narrative steeped in love, trust, respect, and honor of your inner Divinity.

As I've often said, causing real change is about shaking up definitions and breaking through boundaries. It's about elevating and disrupting the status quo. It's about devoting our hearts to sacred confidence — the kind of confidence that inspires us to be wholly seen and heard.

xxx

Amazing Woman Divine Legacy

When a woman opens the radiance of her heart, all doubts drop away and what remains is the wealth of her spiritual purpose.

And as Joan of Arc's words move us to remember:

We are not afraid! We were born for this!

Marsh Engle

Sacred confidence isn't battling to overcome fear.
Or the need to be fearless before you act.
It's a call to magnify your relationship with trust…
allow trust to naturally neutralize fear…
allow trust to be your greatest ally as you
step into the radiant wealth of your divine legacy.

Exploring the Relationship with Sacred Confidence

The connection with our sacred confidence is deeply personal, particularly for those of us called to express our spiritual purpose. We often encounter agreements that impact our relationship with confidence — most often these agreements originate from belief structures, societal norms and cultural conditioning. This becomes especially evident when we examine the definition of Sacred Confidence in contrast to the more commonly defined conventional confidence. It is crucial to distinguish between the two. Let's explore these distinctions together now.

How Does Sacred Confidence Differ from Conventional Confidence?

Sacred Confidence is a profound and intrinsic form of self-assurance that originates from an intimate relationship with our true creative strength and abilities. This type of confidence is rooted in the acknowledgment of our unique gifts and the innate value we bring to the world. It transcends superficial measures of success and societal expectations, focusing instead on personal authority, authenticity and trust in the expression of our innermost creative callings.

Conventional Confidence, on the other hand, is often taught and measured by external standards and achievements. It is typically associated with societal validation, accomplishments, and the ability to meet or exceed predefined expectations. This form of confidence can be heavily influenced by comparisons to others, material success, and the approval of peers and society at large. While Conventional Confidence serves to provide short-term boosts in self-esteem, it lacks the spiritual depth and strength of sacred confidence.

Let's explore even further…

Self-Informed vs. External Informed
Sacred Confidence is self-informed and is derived from an internal understanding and appreciation of one's creative self. It does not rely on external validation or societal approval.

Conventional Confidence often depends on external factors such as achievements, recognition, and the validation by others.

Inner Foundation vs External Foundation
Sacred Confidence is built on self-awareness, authenticity, and the acceptance of one's giftedness, abilities, and creative strengths.

Conventional Confidence is often based on comparisons, competition, and the fulfillment of external expectations.

Spiritual Power vs External Power
Sacred Confidence streams from spiritual power which ensures it is sustainable and enduring, grounded in personal truth and self-acceptance.

Conventional Confidence may fluctuate with changes in external circumstances and over-identification with perceived successes or failures.

Expansion vs Stagnation
Sacred Confidence encourages continuous personal growth, expansion, creativity, and the exploration of one's untapped potentials without fear of judgment.

Conventional Confidence can often hinder growth by fostering fear of failure, placing a ceiling on the courage to try new things and the need to conform to external standards.

Sacred confidence is a deeply rooted sense of self-assurance that arises from embracing the body, mind, and spirit. It offers a more resilient and spiritually fulfilling path to confidence by emphasizing safety in our body, authenticity in our creativity and expansion of our spiritual purpose.

The Body, Mind and Spirit of Sacred Confidence

Cultivating sacred confidence requires a shift in our perspective, mindset and habits — creating the sacred space for a Radiant Reset — opening the flow of a more enriched and enriching relationship with our spiritual purpose, our Divine Legacy.

One of the most effective ways to achieve this Radiant Reset is through somatic practices. These are holistic approaches that focus on the connection between the body, mind, and spirit.

The following practices promote a sense of inner harmony, self-unity, and a fostering of creative balance. Each practice is designed to uncover and enhance higher feminine esteem and recognition of one's inherent worth.

Honoring the Body
The body is the vessel through which we experience the world. By tuning into our physical sensations, we can honor our bodies, acknowledge our body's wisdom and tap into our body's inherent ability to guide us. This physical awareness lays the foundation for sacred confidence by fostering a deep sense of self-acceptance and trust in our bodily experiences.

Honoring the Mind
To engage and honor the mind promotes mindfulness and presence. By focusing on the present moment, we can access and cultivate a clearer and more compassionate understanding of our thoughts, feelings and emotions. This mental clarity allows for the release of self-judgment and the nurturing of positive self-perceptions, which are essential components of sacred confidence.

Honoring the Spirit
The spirit is the essence of our being, connecting us to something greater than ourselves. By incorporating daily practices that honor our spirit, we can tap into a profound sense of purpose and connection, which enhances our overall sense of sacred confidence and well-being.

Sacred Confidence Practices

By integrating the following somatic practices into daily life, we can cultivate a deeper connection with our body, mind, and spirit, ultimately expanding sacred confidence. This holistic approach to self-care empowers us to live authentically and embrace our spiritual purpose, the uniqueness of our strengths, and the wealth of our abilities.

8 Easy Somatic Practices to Build Sacred Confidence

1. **Deep Breathing**: Begin your day by taking slow, deep breaths. Do the same throughout the day. This practice will calm your nervous system and bring your awareness to the present moment.
2. **Body Scanning**: The body is a source of intuition. By pausing to scan your body and noting any areas of tension you can consciously relax and open the body to more insights and guidance.
3. **Mindful Walking**: Walk slowly and deliberately, while paying special attention to the sensations in your feet and legs. This practice will ground your spiritual energy and deepen your connection with your creativity.
4. **Progressive Muscle Relaxation**: Create time to practice releasing stress from the body. You can do this by tensing and then relaxing each muscle group in the body. If you

are interested to learn more, check out the practice of Yoga Nidra for guidance in methods to support you with this practice.
5. **Grounding Exercises**: As simple as this practice may sound, standing feet flat on the ground, imagining roots extending from your soles into the earth will ground your energy. This grounding will open a flow of insights, ideas, and inspiration.
6. **Tai Chi**: By engaging in slow, flowing movements offered through the practice of Tai Chi you not only enhance balance and coordination, but you bring yourself present and into the moment.
7. **Qigong**: The practice of Qigong brings us to focus on gentle movement and breathing techniques to cultivate energy flow. Energy is vibrancy. The more our bodies open to vibrancy the more open we become to the higher states of spiritual expression.
8. **Somatic Meditation**: Meditate with an emphasis on bodily sensations, allowing thoughts to pass without judgment.

Now Let's Get Started.

As you begin your journey through the pages of THE RADIANT RESET, remember this is your personal experience. The ways you may decide to create your own Radiant Reset — or the ways you individualize or connect with your sacred confidence — are different for everyone. It is a unique, individual path.

Here are five practices to support you in gaining greater value from your experience with this book:

Be willing to feel your feelings. Too often we expend enormous energy running away from or shielding ourselves from feeling — possibly because emotional connection has been misinterpreted as weak or without purpose.

To unlock the fullness of our Sacred Confidence, we must free ourselves from the habit of harsh judgment. Otherwise, the feelings we are denying become locked in our physical body, blocking the wealth of our creativity, wisdom voice, and authentic expression.

As you begin to allow yourself to fully feel your feelings, Sacred Confidence can flow freely. Remember, loving acceptance begins with self-acceptance. And it is self-acceptance that shines a light on the essence of your spiritual purpose.

Set aside sacred time and space. Gift yourself the time and space to experience the content of this book. Give yourself the space to fully experience each chapter, the exercises provided, and journaling practices at your own pace. Devote time for contemplation. Allow yourself to define the Radiant Resets you are called to create.

Dedicate yourself to trust. When Sacred Confidence begins to elevate, there will likely be feelings of expansive energy. You may find yourself feeling restless or your mind may spin with distraction. These are all signs that a Radiant Reset is being activated. Call upon the breathwork practice we spoke of earlier. It will support you in grounding your focus. Devote yourself to trust what you feel and any new insights that arise.

Cultivate stillness. Dedicating time to cultivating stillness and rest is vital for activating Sacred Confidence. Over time stillness and rest fortifies and creates an inner environment steeped in connectedness, awareness, and strength... this not only amplifies Sacred Confidence, but it magnifies the focused power of every action.

And finally, before you immerse yourself in the wealth of each of the following chapters, here is one closing thought to remember:

> *Living our spiritual purpose begins with aligning*
> *our actions, thoughts, and intentions with*
> *the richness of our giftedness and*
> *the sacredness of our callings.*

Amazing Woman Divine Legacy

*We must align with our capacities to
give our gifts to the world.*

*This isn't a time to dim our light…
it's time to trust, know, and receive…
it's time to fully embrace the
radiance of our Divine Legacy.*

It is my prayer that within these pages you will find an unshakable bridge to shift into true sacred confidence and set free potentials you've yet to access… the wisdom you've yet to give voice to… and the passions you've yet to unleash.

Marsh Engle

Dedicated to women on the winding
path to their place in the world.

May you embrace your journey with joyful curiosity
and an unshakable sense of your own sacredness,
recognizing the divine design of your remarkable story.

Trust the wisdom of your heart to light
the path with its unique brilliance.

Rest into the power of your Presence and
your connection with the Divine, feeling it
anchor you in your body, in this moment.

Priscilla Hataway

Chapter 1

From Limitation to Radiance:
Expanding Through Presence

Priscilla Hataway

Presence allows us to gently release the illusion of our limitations and expand into the radiant expression of our heart.

Sedona's red rocks warm me after venturing to my favorite vista. A gentle breeze lovingly wipes the kisses of Father Sun from my face. My tailbone and bare feet create a magnetic connection to Mother Earth as her vibrant energy dances up my body and expands my heart. The echo of my heart beating in time with Mother Sedona and with Mother Earth vibrates my being. Each breath moves in time with these wise women who watch over us all, each breath unveiling the unseen world.

My senses heightened, I hear the songs of birds, the buzz of bees, the rustle of lizards and quiet grace of grazing deer. Colors seem so saturated in the special way twilight reveals herself to this canyon, creating a watercolor wash of oranges, pinks and yellows, while the sun slips behind the mountains to bless another horizon with his inspiring light.

> *In these moments of true connection and presence,*
> *I find alignment and centeredness,*
> *a place of rest in my true nature.*

Grounded in the present moment, my entire being resets, vital to reclaiming a balanced, loving, and wondrous life. I move through each day thinking how miraculous it is to be *this* Spirit, partnering with *this* body on *this* planet, at *this* time, creating *this* radical story named Priscilla. I look forward to the creative ways life unfolds, knowing that Presence invites Life to play, and the possibilities are infinite. When faced with challenges, I think "how interesting" as I surrender the story and await the revelation.

> *In Presence, we experience a sense of wholeness,*
> *completeness, and a quiet power,*
> *cradling our unique essence within us.*

We walk in intimate connection with our bodies, a deep Knowing residing in our hearts. We are in a state of peaceful activation, seeing the world as it is while carrying a Mona Lisa smile. We hold our energy close, nurturing it with wisdom and self-love, guiding it toward its most potent expression. We create and choose from the deep well of body wisdom, not the impulsive reactions of fear or the sway of emotions.

In the heart of Presence, we can Love everything as Creation loves Possibility. We move into the liminal spaces of existence and magnetize magic to our everyday moments. Resting into an empowered partnership with All That Is, we release the need to struggle, feeling how we are held by the Universe.

When we sit back in Presence and admire the wonderful way the world works without us interfering, we are allowing the world to show itself to us. We can observe Life and get to know it for what it is, beyond our desire to change it. We learn to release our questions to the universe, trusting that the answers will find their way back to us in perfect timing.

> *The radiant reset, grounded in Presence,*
> *invites us to release the familiar*
> *and step into a life we never dared to dream,*
> *a life more beautiful and authentic*
> *than we could have imagined.*

Looking back, I can see that Presence has been the guiding force quietly orchestrating the synchronicities that have defined my path. My journey hasn't followed any traditional formula for manifestation. The most meaningful parts of my life came to me in unexpected ways and at unexpected times. With a Master's in Business and twelve years in the corporate world, I never envisioned myself in the healing arts, let alone owning a sound healing studio in Sedona, Arizona. Resisting the call to start my own business for several years, I finally answered just days before COVID-19 shut down the world and life profoundly transformed.

My healing practice has flourished organically for five years, without any marketing efforts. The opportunity to purchase my sound healing studio happened unexpectedly, the seller repeatedly offered better terms, without me asking, just to do something kind.

*I never imagined I could live
such a magical and fulfilling life.
I didn't feel ready or deserving.
The secret wasn't hard work or struggle,
but the quiet power of Presence.*

But the more I surrendered to trust, the more I embraced the path before me, honoring my gifts and stepping into my destiny. I still never know what's next, but I've experienced enough synchronicity and flow to trust a divine design beyond my comprehension. Instead of trying to control my life, I'm fascinated by what Creation brings my way. Over time, I've become more practiced at knowing when to let go and make space for something more. I've learned that Presence isn't something we achieve; it's a journey of expansion, a blossoming of our being. Each step, each expansion, reveals new depths and brings me closer to the heart of Presence.

The First Expansion
*Presence was the key,
unraveling heavy layers
of perceived worth
to reveal the radiant truth
of all that I am.
It was a shift from doing to being.*

Coming Home to Ourselves
I was utterly exhausted, stretched thin between a new baby and a new business. My innate desire to do everything right was in hyperdrive, leaving my nervous system constantly on edge. I was so disconnected from my life, unable to truly

appreciate the wonderful things happening around me. I knew something had to change, but I couldn't grasp how to end the cycle I was in. During a healing session with a client, I received a divinely inspired message that resonated with both of us.

My efforts to avoid being abandoned by over-serving everyone else led me to abandon myself. The resulting stress and loneliness were a constant reminder of this self-betrayal, and they wouldn't go away until I turned my focus inward.

As women, we often feel called to be all things to everyone and our generous hearts want to do just that. We have been told that to get the life we want, we must continuously improve, strive for more, and be better than we thought we could be. In this quest to become what the world says we need to be, we've lost touch with simply being ourselves. The longing we feel isn't for a checklist of accomplishments but for the daily experience of love, completeness, happiness, and fulfillment. These feelings aren't contingent on a partner, career, children, or wealth. While these external factors can be tools in our journey, ultimately, we are called to cultivate these feelings within our own hearts.

Instead of believing I was the sole solution for everything and everyone, I began to take a step back and watch life happening around me. I began asking more questions instead of supplying all the answers. At first, it was almost offensive how well the world worked without me managing it. It dawned on me that the 'perfect' image I was striving for was one I had created for myself. In the life I was living now, I was the only one insisting I had to have it all together and be everyone's savior. Suddenly, I could believe I was loved and valued just for being me, regardless of whether I was constantly helping or organizing. I discovered that stepping back made space for others to step up and feel empowered. Letting go created space in my mind, allowing for deeper rest and a greater focus on connecting with my body.

As I consistently prioritized my own well-being and allowed others to support me, I began to feel at home in my life again, finally experiencing a sense of safety and ease.

For more than ten years, I've facilitated journeys of self-discovery, helping people connect with their life purpose. Utilizing deep hypnosis, we create a bridge to their own infinite wisdom, seeking answers from within. Despite the diverse backgrounds and experiences of those I work with, the message is consistent:

*Your life's purpose is the journey to your most authentic self —
a deep connection that allows you to remember who you truly are.*

Presence is the art of becoming, the counterpart to process. It's not about doing but being. Within Presence, there is wisdom, ease, grace, unconditional love — a softness. Presence has substance, steadiness, open arms, and an open heart. It's what you carry within you, what others feel in your presence.

Ultimately, it's what people connect to and remember — not what you do or say, but how you make them feel.

As I shed the layers of what I thought gave me worth, I began a deep and loving relationship with my true self. I embraced both my shadow and light, engaging in heartfelt conversations with the complex mosaic of women who live within me. I embraced my desire to experience all facets of life, recognizing it as a strength, a superpower, not as a sign of being lost. I was learning to cherish all that I am.

The Second Expansion
Releasing the belief that my mind defined me
and embracing my identity
as a spirit lovingly guiding this human body,
allowed me to find true empowerment through Presence.

Awakening To Our Power
Initially, awakening to my power looked like taking charge — mastering my thoughts, feelings, and nervous system to feel safe. We are wired to believe understanding equals safety, but this quest inevitably leads to burnout and anxiety.

Because we have such busy minds,
we often define ourselves by our
thoughts and feelings,
labeling ourselves anxious, overthinkers, analytical —
forgetting the eternal, centered
and peaceful nature of our true selves.

My blend of strong intuition and sharp logic, both strong forces, often leads to mental overload. I tell myself that my curiosity and intelligence *should* be enough to find answers through logic and reasoning. I also tell myself that my intuition *should* naturally guide me, given my connection to the unseen world. I have overused both sides of my mind in a loving effort to feel safe for a long time. And I've struggled to get out of the spiral of stories the mind creates.

A few years ago, in meditation, I received "*A Blueprint for Being Human,*" a divinely inspired framework I now share with clients. It was pivotal, transforming my understanding of my body, its capabilities, and how to work with energy.

> *I relinquished the illusion of being my body*
> *and embraced the role of loving guide,*
> *a "big sister spirit" shepherding it*
> *through its first human experience.*
> *This relationship transformed*
> *into a collaborative journey*
> *with my body, walking hand in hand.*

I saw the amazing tools within — the logical mind's library, the intuitive mind's vision, the feeling heart, the instinctual belly, and more. Like any council, each had a divine purpose and perspective, but no singular part of me held the entire truth. As this "big sister spirit" or higher self, I also had a big-picture perspective to lend to the body as its guide.

It was a gradual awakening: my mind wasn't designed to be a master of the universe — understanding and controlling everything. Its true power lies in creating sensory memories of the present moment, memories I can use to embody Presence. These memories can even evoke specific energies, aligning me with my desired state of being. Recalling the feeling of delight, for instance, instantly shifts me back into that delicious state. In this spirit of newfound partnership, I spoke to my mind: "Sweet Mind, thank you for your tireless efforts to keep me safe. We both believed this was your sole purpose, but I now understand that safety exists even amidst uncertainty. I won't ask you to do the impossible. Instead, I have a far more powerful role for you to play."

I spoke to every part of my body, creating connections with the unique tools and energies within. I shifted from seeing these energies as adversaries to embracing them as allies, approaching them with compassion.

I came to more fully embrace my body as sacred and beautiful, as something I have been given the holy task of caring for. This shift cultivated a deep softness and open-heartedness toward my humanity, awakening within me even greater love, grace, and empowerment.

The Third Expansion
*The most challenging part of my journey
to wholeness hasn't been
healing where I was broken,
it has been learning ways to celebrate my gifts.*

Claiming Our Sacredness

We often take our natural gifts for granted, assuming that what comes easily isn't special. It can be frightening to see ourselves as beautiful, sacred beings worthy of love and admiration. This fear became palpable on a hike with friends, when I felt a wave of nervousness as I prepared to share some exciting news. Their genuine joy triggered embarrassment, and I felt myself shrinking back.

> *I felt my body pushing away all this*
> *love and gratitude for who I am.*
> *At that moment, I said a prayer.*
> *"Show me all the amazing parts of myself*
> *that I have not felt safe enough to see."*

In an instant, I was flooded with images — hundreds of television screens displaying different moments of my life, both big and small. As I allowed these images into my heart, a wave of emotion washed over me. A gentle voice spoke, *"This is just a whisper of all the wonderful things that you are."*

> *The truth had finally landed in my heart:*
> *we can only embrace the love we believe we deserve.*
> *My deepening love affair with myself has become*
> *a gateway for receiving love from others and*
> *overflowing with love for all that surrounds me.*

Since that day, I have made it a practice to celebrate the good things about myself. Each time it gets more and more comfortable to hold space with my own brilliance.

Now my young daughter and I share this beautiful ritual, taking a few moments each day to celebrate three things we cherish about ourselves, a tender act of self-love.

The experience of Presence, with its inherent sense of wonder, opens the door to a deeper understanding of sacredness. When we see life through this lens, we recognize the inherent meaning and purpose of everything in existence. We move beyond judging the world based on its impact on us; while still embracing how interconnected we are within this beautiful tapestry. Each element, from the smallest microbe to the largest star, plays a vital role in the grand design, and we, as humans, are integral threads within it, not separate from it.

*The belief in inherent sacredness naturally leads to
an unconditional form of love.
When we see the divine spark in everything,
we can love more freely,
without judgment or conditions.*

Loving acceptance allows us to process our emotions, learn from our experiences, and move forward with greater peace and resilience. It encourages us to see the innate magic in all things, to embrace the present moment, and to express compassion for ourselves and others. As we reach even more profound levels of safety in our bodies, we can shift our focus inward, cultivating Presence.

By investing energy in noticing and nurturing our strengths — courage, creativity, brilliance — we foster a more authentic and powerful sense of self.

With this new habit of positivity, gratitude, and self-care, anything needing healing will naturally arise to be loved and held. We no longer need to constantly seek out flaws to fix; we simply love what emerges and allow it to heal. Through sacredness and acceptance, I moved beyond traditional healing models of processing thoughts and feelings. I reclaimed my life through self-love, embodiment, and connection, finally enjoying being myself, being in my body, and feeling safe to seek deeper connections with others.

The Fourth Expansion
*Connection brings all of our senses
into the present moment.
This is where we create a vivid experience of living.*

Weaving Connection
Presence relies on both grounding and connection because it is through these two anchors that we find our true place in the world, both rooted and reaching. When we are grounded, we are connected to the earth, to our bodies, and to the present moment. It helps us to call back our energy, returning to ourselves and to the here and now. When we are grounded, we are more in tune with our intuition and inner wisdom because we are not relying solely on thought and emotion. From this centeredness, we can listen to other sources of wisdom within us.

*Grounding is where we engage
all of our senses to see the world
through the lens of our body's experience.
We get out of our head and into our humanity.*

Connection reminds us that we are not alone. We are part of a larger web of life, interconnected with all beings and the world around us. This sense of connection can bring a deep sense of belonging and purpose. It allows us to share our lives with others, to give and receive love, and to experience the joy of human interaction. It also opens us up to the natural world and to the Divine, to whatever it is that's older and bigger than us — the unseen force holds the template for our own complexity.

*My sacred partnership with the Divine
strengthens my human connections,
reminding me that grounding and connection
are not mutually exclusive.
In fact, they enhance each other.*

Engaging more fully with the earth and my body brought strength and security, allowing for more authentic connections with others. Genuine connection reinforces my sense of self and belonging, reminding me I'm held and supported by a web of relationships, both physical and spiritual. This safety allows me to move from fear to faith, to slow down and trust, to release hyper-vigilance, and to observe. I can feel myself as part of All That Is, shifting my identity, perceptions, and therefore, my reality.

The Fifth Expansion
The Sacred Pause is a powerful tool
on the path to Presence.
It's in those moments,
after we've done all we know how to do,
that we are invited to simply be with what is.

Stepping into Stillness

The Sacred Pause is a magical space where we witness divine love in action. It's where we can release control and allow existence to reorganize itself to meet our deepest needs, trusting that our plans may not be the whole story. We experience a pause in action and an openness of the heart.

The Sacred Pause gives us the space to find the grace
to understand and do our best with what we know.
It's a place to recognize the cycles of creativity,
knowing when doing ends and being begins.

Moving into my adulthood, I held specific ideas of security and success. Working and studying full-time, I graduated high school early and began college right away. Life took many unexpected turns — multiple car accidents, 9/11, a catastrophic hurricane, and the 2008 economic crash — but I continued to strive for a traditional life. By the time I graduated with my Masters, I'd attended colleges in five states and worked in seven industries.

I strived to do the "right" things, yet security and success always seemed just out of reach. It became comical how quickly my life cycled between highs and lows beyond my control. The Sacred Pause would unexpectedly intervene, and in its quiet embrace, I explored Presence and its ever-deepening experience. While waiting for the path forward to become clear, I turned inward, healing, offering compassion to my fears, held by the deep knowing that I was part of a divine plan beyond my comprehension.

*Looking back on the first two decades of my career,
I was always fulfilling my purpose.
I was a healing presence,
placed in crisis situations not as punishment,
but so the best parts of me could be revealed.*

I was always being who I was meant to be, building resilience in the process. Having stability might have prevented me from cultivating self-reliance and a deep connection to the Divine. I might have surrendered my power, robbing me of the strength and self-assurance I have now. I might not have had the faith for the massive leaps the next phase of my life required — faith that allowed me to move to Sedona, become a mother, and share my sacred work.

Each of *The Five Expansions* ushered me into a life of tremendous depth, meaning, purpose and wonder and I know there are still more expansions for me to discover. The beauty of doing this work is remembering that you don't have to have it all figured out in order to share your own wisdom and let it have value to the world. Someone is ready to hear exactly what you have to say just the way you say it. Someone is waiting to see the way you move through life and be inspired by it. Someone is waiting to feel your Presence, just as it is today and feel the call to go deeper into themselves.

Stepping into my calling to help others connect with their inner wisdom has been the most profound journey of my life — a masterclass in empowerment, self-love, and the reclamation of my authentic self. And this is what I long for you to experience: that with each step on your path, you discover new and unexpected ways to accept and embrace the truth that you are on the right path. May your body become a sacred haven for your ever-expanding spirit. May you find rest in the unwavering truth of your own power, your inherent sacredness.

And as you revel in the radiance of your unique heart, may you join me in this daily prayer: *"What beautiful possibilities have I not yet imagined? Universe, send me that!"*

Radiant Reset Journaling

The following journaling prompts will guide you on a journey to cultivate Presence. Each prompt will explore *The Five Expansions*, revealing how Presence helps you gently release the illusion of limitations and expand into the radiant expression of your heart.

Before diving into each prompt, take a few deep breaths and center yourself.

As you consider the question, notice any physical sensations or emotional responses. You might even place a hand on your heart or belly to connect more deeply with your body's wisdom. Practice inviting and receiving answers — imagine the information flowing to you, rather than you having to figure it out. Trust the insights that arise

Expansion 1
Coming Home to Ourselves

What does my "most authentic self" look and feel like? What steps can I take to embody this self more fully?

_____
_____
_____
_____
_____
_____
_____
_____
_____
_____
_____
_____
_____
_____

AMAZING WOMAN DIVINE LEGACY

Expansion 2
Awakening to Our Power

How can I utilize my mind's ability to create sensory memories to support my well-being? What sensory memories bring me joy, peace, or presence?

_____
_____
_____
_____
_____
_____
_____
_____
_____
_____
_____
_____
_____
_____

AMAZING WOMAN DIVINE LEGACY

Expansion 3
Claiming Ourselves as Sacred

If I were to invite in a "television screen" montage of all the wonderful parts of myself that I've been unable to celebrate, what images arise? What do these images tell me about my radiant heart? How can I become even more comfortable sitting with my own brilliance?

AMAZING WOMAN DIVINE LEGACY

Expansion 4
Weaving Connection

How has my understanding of myself and my place in the world evolved through these experiences of grounding, connection, and Presence?

_____
_____
_____
_____
_____
_____
_____
_____
_____
_____
_____
_____
_____

AMAZING WOMAN DIVINE LEGACY

Expansion 5
Stepping into Stillness

How does the Sacred Pause help me to "simply be with what is"? What does this "being" feel like?

_____
_____
_____
_____
_____
_____
_____
_____
_____
_____
_____
_____
_____
_____
_____
_____

AMAZING WOMAN DIVINE LEGACY

About Priscilla Hataway

As a Sound Alchemist and Divine Channel, Priscilla Hataway brings voice and presence to the wisdom and compassion of higher consciousness, sharing new frequencies to uplift our world. She offers private retreats, group teachings, and sacred sound and guided meditation experiences in her West Sedona studio, at private locations, and in nature. Priscilla also facilitates online transformational spiritual healing sessions, guiding others to experience the profound power of Presence and connect with their own inner wisdom for deep and lasting healing.

As a passionate spiritual seeker and teacher, she is dedicated to helping people discover their paths toward a greater connection to themselves and the Divine. Always an intuitive child, her Divine Channel opened wide at the age of 12. Suddenly, she was having prophetic dreams, speaking in unknown languages and her hands would heat up with healing energy. By the age of 14, she was struggling to feel an alignment with the systems and adults attempting to guide her, so she decided to take a step back and be a normal teenager. She went on to study business and law in college and started her corporate career. Even though she maintained a special intuitive sense and connection to something bigger than her, Priscilla didn't fully return to her gifts until her late 20s.

She shares, *"I felt I had done all the things the world said should make me happy, but something was still missing. It was time to see what I could salvage from my childhood experiences, add wisdom from many spiritual traditions and find a newfound freedom in my spiritual path to make it my own."*

Becoming a mother expanded my heart and led me to an even deeper level of personal healing. Having to teach someone else to be human brings an acute awareness of how our beliefs, identities, and perceptions are created. It allowed me to inventory and be present with the unconscious tools I no longer needed to feel safe.

My calling is to share what I have learned and experienced to help others find their truth, freedom, and connection. Whatever your spiritual journey looks like, I am here to help guide you and support you along the way."

For more information about Priscilla Hataway and her transformational healing work, visit: PriscillaHataway.com

To experience sacred sound, visit
Sacred Rememberings — Sound Healing in Sedona, Arizona
SacredRememberings.com

Dedicated to the women who dare to put pen to paper,
who weave their truths into words,
and who give voice to the untold — this is for you.

May you write boldly, without apology.
May your stories find the light they deserve.
May your words heal, inspire, and ignite change.

The world needs your voice, your perspective,
your history, and your dreams.
Keep writing. Keep sharing.
Keep making space for yourself and others.

This is your story — as only you can tell it.

Diane Sova

Chapter 2

Whispers from the Past:
Wisdom for the Future

Diane Sova

On many levels, we add value and meaning to our lives by sharing stories, the touchstones of our divine legacy.

One afternoon, as I waited for a friend in the retirement home he'd just moved to, a woman shuffled by pushing her walker. Her head was bowed and her shoulders slumped, but I noticed several medals hanging by ribbons from the front bar. Gently I asked, "Excuse me, would you tell me about these medals?"

She immediately straightened, pulling her shoulders up by a good two inches. "I won these for championship swimming!" More surprising than the statement was the sparkle that came into her eyes, "But no one cares anymore." I gestured towards a nearby bench, asking, "Do you have a minute to tell me more?"

We had a fascinating, lively chat. When my friend arrived, I introduced them, mentioning a few tidbits about each to break the ice and keep the conversation going. The swimmer was 93, my friend 92. We had lunch together in the main dining room that day and they have since become great friends. Every time I see her, she thanks me for paying attention, bringing her story to life again, and introducing her to new friends.

> *Her untold story and her loneliness pierced my heart.*
> *When we tell our stories and listen to others,*
> *not only do we connect to one another,*
> *we open hearts and celebrate lives.*

My own great-grandmother, Rhoda Leoda Collins, was a huge part of my younger life. Born in 1888, she entertained us kids with wild tales of growing up in western Canada. She met and married the love of her life, an immigrant from Ireland named Freeman Congleton, then moved with him to Upper Michigan. He was a lumberjack; she their camp cook. Imagine being the only woman in a lumberjack camp for months on end! One of her stories was about Freeman getting the end of his nose bitten off during a fight with a Wisconsin lumberjack. Fights were a common form of entertainment among woodsmen in the north, burning off steam and easing loneliness. With no doctors even remotely nearby, she tended his wound, wrapping a woolen sock around his face until his knubby nose healed somewhat.

They had three children. It wasn't until those children were fully grown with families of their own that we learned our great-great grandfather Freeman Congleton wasn't a true Congleton at all — he was born a Beardsley! His parents died on the ship coming over from Ireland. His newly married older sister was also on the ship with her young husband —

named Congleton. They hurriedly adopted Freeman before arriving in Canada. With that adoption, Freeman Beardsley became Freeman Congleton — and all his descendants were Congletons! Our family didn't stem from whence we thought.

Our lives matter. Stories live on through the ages.

My great-grandmother's stories remain with me to this day, and it tugs my heart to realize that I am the last generation to know her. When she passed at age 88, there were many more questions I wished I'd asked. What was her favorite treat as a child? When did she first ride in a car? How did she feel getting into that mechanical marvel? Where was her first child born? What kind of furniture did she have? We never wrote her stories down, never captured her joys and sorrows, the wonderment and curiosity of her youth. She was an archivist of pain and resilience — a keeper of ancestral wisdom. It was opportunity lost, with no chance of ever knowing.

I learned from that lost opportunity and bought a journal for my maternal grandmother when she was in her late 80s, so she could write down her stories for the family. I called her to make sure she'd received it, saying, "Grandma, if you'd take fifteen minutes a day to write down your stories, we'll have them to keep forever!" She replied, "Well, Diane, if you'd take fifteen minutes a day to call me, I'd tell you all my stories." She had me there.

Over the years, I've gathered hundreds of fascinating stories. I find that elders have so much to share, from wild times in their youth to survival and wisdom gained as they aged. They lived through what we know as history, loving passionately, drowning in sorrow, always working for better tomorrows.

Stories carry the power to transport us to another time and place. They help us forget about our current surroundings or situations, allowing us to become immersed in another reality. Storytelling provides us all an opportunity to preserve memories and wisdom. Research has shown that chemicals are released in the brain as people both tell and listen to stories. They become lighter and happier and especially realize that their life stories are worth sharing and preserving. The story becomes medicine for both the storyteller and the listener.

Every era, every life has its own magic.
It's just a matter of finding it.

Many of the elders I sought out had no family around and as they aged, had become isolated without many friends or visitors. My mission became meeting and hearing people, connecting with them in ways that they felt valued, respected, and loved, knowing that their life was significant enough that someone cared. For all of us, recalling and contemplating memorable experiences can generate a sense of purpose, providing reassurance, self-understanding, validation, and clarity. I want all of us to honor our elders and share their stories, to connect them with others that will also honor and value them. I want people to realize their significance in our world and to know that their life has meaning. It comes through connecting and getting to know them through their stories.

*In times of transition,
especially towards the end of life,
story sharing holds the power
of illuminating a path forward,
providing a sense of purpose
and a reason to continue.
This provides an immeasurable
sense of serenity and closure.*

There was Mr. James, in his mid-90s, introduced to me by his home care nurse. When I asked him to share a little bit about his life, he asked why. "Because your stories are important, Mr. James. They're part of who we are. And who knows, maybe sharing your story will help others feel a little less lonely." His eyes, usually clouded with a stoic indifference, gleamed with something akin to pride. Sometimes all people need is an invitation and a little encouragement to open up.

At first, his answers were brief, almost dismissive, but with each question, his words grew more elaborate, painting vivid pictures of a time long past. His voice cracked with emotion as he spoke of his comrades during WW1, his eyes misting over as he recounted tales of valor and loss. There was a transformation in Mr. James as he spoke. The stern lines of his face softened, and a glimpse of the young man he once was shone through. I felt a pang of empathy, realizing the weight of untold stories he must have carried all these years. His was a story that needed to be told, a legacy that deserved to be preserved. His stories painted a rich tapestry of life, love, and loss that helped shape the community where he'd lived. At one point, we talked about his family. "It's been a while since I talked about my wife," he admitted. "Seems like everyone but me has forgotten her."

"We won't forget her," I promised. "And neither will anyone else who hears your story." I couldn't help but feel I'd made a small but significant difference in Mr. James' life. Our elders have so much wisdom and history, and it's all just… slipping away. I know all too well how time has a way of eroding the vividness of even the most cherished moments.

We are blessed to know people by way of their stories.

With a thirst for knowledge and a love for hearing stories, I set out on a journey to uncover the hidden gems of wisdom and experience that our elders possess. I approached other residents, each with their own treasure trove of memories. There was Mrs. Groswild, whose vivid recollections of her town's more colorful past painted a picture of a place far different from the city it had become. She had a penchant for telling tales, juicy stories of speakeasies and dance halls, of love affairs that scandalized the town, and of quiet moments of friendship that had seen her through the hardest of times. Her laughter was infectious, and her eyes sparkled with mischief as she regaled me with stories of her youth. We had a great time together.

Another precious encounter was with Mrs. Jenkins. She invited me to come sit down and shared with me stories of her childhood during the great depression and her later challenges and struggles as a young single mother. She told me about the utter desolation she felt after the loss of her husband and how she felt so alone and unable to cope. Then more stories about how she found solace among kindred spirits sharing similar griefs along life's winding paths. She met with other widows at her church and gradually felt alive again, even traveling the world and experiencing new adventures in her golden years.

There was Mr. Patel, in his late 80s when we met, whose journey from India as a teenager to a small town in the Midwest was a testament to bravery, courage, love, and his quest for a better life. A retired professor with a sharp mind and a kind heart, he spoke of his passion for teaching and his love for his late wife, who he described as his perfect soulmate. He also imparted valuable lessons on the importance of education for our youth and the power of perseverance in the face of challenge, for people of all ages.

I must mention Gene, one of the founders of an aerospace research center before the space age was even considered possible. He had some amazing tales of a rich life full of surprises, living until he was 103. We became close friends over the years. He once told me that he wanted to live longer than his brother, who was 107 when he passed! Gene was unique in that he gathered his family's extensive history over the years and captured their stories in several volumes. His was a fascinating journey, traversing time with him to learn of long-ago adventures.

Gene studied physics back east and earned his PhD before moving west to work for Hughes Aircraft. He met and married his wife after college; they had two children. It was in the 1950s when he packed them up in his Chevrolet for the drive to California. He had me in stitches, talking about their adventures (and misadventures) along the way. By the time I met Gene, his wife was gone. He'd spent seven years caring for her by himself, even when she no longer recognized him or knew who he was. Talk about lonely! It was a long, sad period for him. His love, respect, and memories of their 60+ years together where all that sustained him. He thoroughly enjoyed our times together reminiscing and said that sharing his stories brought a 'breath of fresh air' back into his life.

I also spoke with Mr. Casteneda, in his early 80s, about his family's immigration from Mexico and the challenges they faced building a new life here in the U.S. amidst outright prejudice and deject poverty. I met Mrs. Lee, who told of her family's struggles and survival (or not) during the Korean War, and the joy she eventually found after migrating to her new home in San Francisco.

> *All these storytellers share a common thread —*
> *resilience of the human spirit*
> *and the quiet heroism found in everyday lives.*

Their stories varied in tone and topic, but all of them shared a common thread: the resilience of the human spirit and the quiet heroism found in everyday lives. Each interview was a delicate dance, coaxing out the moments of joy and sorrow that had shaped their characters. Every story I recorded wove a thread of camaraderie and caring, pieces of a puzzle that revealed a picture of perseverance against all odds, resilience in bouncing back, deep love, and tight-knit community. The seniors began looking forward to being interviewed, eager to share their lives with someone who truly cared. Their stories turned into catalysts for connection, their spirits undiminished by the passing years.

What transformation in our society could we bring about when individuals are heard, supported, and nurtured while sharing their stories?

The stories I heard were threads woven together in a colorful tapestry of life. I was fascinated by the different perspectives, the trials and triumphs, and the lessons learned along the way. The people behind the stories were what truly captivated me. Their wrinkles hold a lifetime of experiences, their eyes sparkle with memories, and their voices are filled with wisdom.

Through my interactions, I learned that life is a journey filled with highs and lows, but it's the lessons we learn and the people we meet that make it all worthwhile. I learned the value of patience, empathy, humor, and the importance of cherishing every moment. As I said my goodbyes to each newfound friend, I couldn't help but feel grateful for the time they had given me and the stories they shared.

As elders, I see them as the keepers of a treasure trove of knowledge and experiences that I will carry with me for the rest of my life.

I had an idea to further connect people across ages, backgrounds, educations. Middle school students would choose an elderly resident in their area to interview, learn about their life, and document their stories. The students connected with their neighbors — and even their relatives — getting to know them as real people. History came alive through these intimate conversations — and so did the old folks! The students learned of the grit that shaped their town's soul.

It makes a difference. The idea of capturing moments and memories for posterity not only brings joy to the lives of the elderly but can bridge the gap between neighbors who may have lived side by side for years without truly knowing each other. On many levels, everyone benefits.

Magic happens when people engage
their inner world (their stories) with the outer world.

The saddest moments in my life have been when a person is near their end of life, dying with their song unsung, their story untold. I learned that it's never too late…unless you wait. One day, I too will be long forgotten, merely a name on a family tree somewhere, my passions, talents, adventures, and even my personality gone to dust. It tugs my heart, knowing that our ancestors were real people, once alive with emotions and experiences just as we have today. We never want to think of our grandparents or even our parents falling in love, having hot, passionate sex, or crying of a broken heart… but they did! And when I think of how many ancestors it took to create us, we are fortunate to even be here. Think: only ten generations back, we had 2,046 ancestors in our direct family tree. What were their lives like? What stories would they have told?

> *I made it my mission to pass along the touchstones*
> *and whispers from the past,*
> *ensuring that the stories of our ancestors*
> *— and our own stories —*
> *would never be forgotten.*

Creating a library of our elder's histories, capturing their memories and stories into perpetuity not only for us, but for future generations, has become a mission of my life. When children and grandchildren learn about their ancestors, they learn about themselves, developing a sense of pride in who they are and where they came from.

> *Stories can also heal generational trauma.*
> *But be warned…*
> *some stories bear scars deeper than skin.*

Generational trauma is the passing of traumatic experiences or traits from one generation to the next. It begins with direct experiences, like witnessing acts of violence or living where the threat of violence is ever present. For example, children who grow up in homes with alcoholism, domestic violence, and childhood trauma may pass those experiences to the next generation — after all, that's how they grew up; they never knew anything different. The cycle of unresolved traumas can affect multiple generations to come.

Diane Sova

So often we miss out on the opportunity
to see our elders as real people.
It is through honoring them for their humanness
that we learn the breadth
and depth of their life experiences.
We grow from knowing them to stand
in the true power of our heritage.

These are our roots. The pain we carry is not ours alone; it was woven into our lineage. When we share these stories — the trials endured by our ancestors and their survival through them — we stitch together patches from our shared history into quilts that can warm even the coldest hearts. By sharing stories, individuals and their experiences are humanized, making it easier for others to relate and empathize.

What is the power in sharing your story? When we hide, avoid, or bury certain parts of ourselves, it is because we fear that someone will judge, criticize, or even reject us. This is often lonely and exhausting. By openly sharing our stories, we foster connections and create environments where solitude and secrecy give way to solidarity and support.

I believe the strongest word
in the English language is perception.
What we seek or perceive is what we see and believe.
Consequently, we can expand or diminish
the true power of our life experiences.
If we have a limited view of our ancestors' lives,
we can easily assume those same limitation in our own life.

Through conversations with my maternal grandmother, my mother, my cousins, and my aunts, I was astounded to learn of family secrets that had been borne through generations. As I delved deeper into my family's history, I began to understand the root of our generation's pain. I saw my grandparents and parents in a new light, empathizing with the struggles they faced. And most importantly, I realized that I was not alone in struggles with my own family. With newfound understanding and compassion, our extended family was able to connect on a deeper level. We finally understood that our parents and grandparents weren't harboring secrets, in their minds, they were protecting us from truths we weren't ready to face. We began sharing stories and memories, and for the first time, acknowledged the pain, shame, and secrets that had been hidden for so long. Together, we are beginning to heal and break free from the chains of our past.

It is through stories we discover generational wounds that are asking to be healed.

My grandmother's grandfather was alcoholic and beat his wife (her grandmother) harshly and often. No one ever spoke of it, but sometimes family gatherings at their farm were canceled amidst whispers of events. Their children witnessed the violence and drinking that was always present, but they never, ever spoke of what went on at home.

My grandmother's own father drank, beat her mother, and was a known womanizer. They had five children. When their young son died of pneumonia at 3 years old, my grandfather blamed her. He beat her half to death, then left her for another woman. With four young daughters to care for on her own and no support or money coming in, she cleaned houses and cooked at a local eatery. This was my great-grandmother. I only met her a few times and my great-grandfather twice. He was blind when my family visited and didn't trust the food given to him — only his whiskey. He was frightening to me even then, young as I was.

One of their daughters was my grandmother. She studied to become a teacher, the first in the family to receive an education. Young and determined to make a better life for herself, she married a promising, attractive local boy… who also turned out to be a violent, drunken womanizer. He moved her away from her family — nearly 1000 miles to the north, where she knew no one. She was the first in the family to ever move away and her remaining three sisters missed her terribly. The young couple was desperately poor; both had grown up that way. They had three children together, a boy and two girls. My grandfather got a job as a baker. His work at the bakery required him to be up at 3:30 am, so my grandma got up early every morning to fix him breakfast. Often, he stopped at a local bar on his way home from work and slapped her around if he came home and the children were making any noise at all.

My mother remembers seeing her mother crying into a pillow, hiding her face from them. This was during the depression years. One day, her father (my grandfather) didn't come home at all, leaving them with little food and no money. He was gone for a couple of weeks, then one day brought a woman to the house to pick up his things. He told my grandma that she needed to meet 'a real woman.' How traumatizing that must have been! Thankfully my grandmother eventually divorced him — another first for the family. To survive, following the footsteps of her own mother, she took in boarders and cleaned houses. At one point, she even put her children in a welfare home so she could work an outside job.

Their daughters were my mother and my aunt. My own father was never physically abusive, but he was alcoholic and terrorized our family. My aunt's husband was also a drunk, violent and physically abusive. To this day, our family is terribly dysfunctional. Of five children in my immediate family, four have been married and divorced multiple times; one never married at all. I first married young, to a sweet farm boy I met in 4H. He beat me repeatedly, beginning on the first night of our honeymoon in a tent at an isolated camping spot. Each time, he swore he was sorry and would never do it again. The shame and humiliation were overwhelming — and I never spoke of it to my family. Unbeknownst to me at the time, this was carrying on our family's generational pattern! It wasn't until after I escaped and divorced him and after both my father and uncle died that I learned just how prevalent the pattern of marrying alcoholic, violent men was in our extended family line.

We all have our own LEGACY STORY… passed from prior generations of strong and resilient men and women.

The question is: Can we rewrite our story?

Hearing the stories and learning the truth about my elders and their lives has helped heal those of my generation. We can finally see and understand the challenges and the strength of our grandparents and parents. By talking and speaking the truth, we are healing such memories, changing our own lives and those of our future generations. There is power in knowing.

There is another part of this. We have the ability to rewrite our stories! Re-telling and reinterpreting those stories can empower and even transform our lives. Rewriting your life story is a process of finding meaning in your life events, recognizing the growth and learning that has shaped you, and changing your perspective. Below are some steps you can take to rewrite your life story:

1. **Write:** In 20 minutes or less, write down the most meaningful moments in your life; events, relationships, work you did, or things you've learned.
2. **Identify your story's theme:** Read through your story, noting and identifying the most common recurring verbs, situations, and themes.
3. **Name your story:** Choose a name that matches the story you've written.
4. **Now change your theme:** A "theme" is the underlying message or central idea of a story, often exploring universal concepts like love, courage, loss, redemption, or the nature of good versus evil; it's the deeper meaning of a story, not just the surface-level events.
5. Consider what **theme** you'd prefer your story to have, and what new name you'd give it if it were a book or movie.

6. **Rewrite your story:** What would your story look like from a different perspective? Try on a new theme — or perhaps a few!
7. **Reflect:** Set the new story aside for a couple of days, then read it again. Rewrite and continue rewriting until you own your new version and vision.

Rewriting your life story is not about denying your past or being delusional, but rather about how changing your perception of events or people's actions helps heal trauma and woundedness, adding new meaning and understanding to your life.

My ultimate mission is to get people connected and talking. Let's all become connection catalysts!

One thing I see desperately missing in our world is connection — with our history, our inner selves, our physical world, our divine destiny, with each other. I bridge those worlds and am committed to nurturing and helping people overcome obstacles, tapping into their creativity to rewrite their stories and cultivate their sense of community and belonging.

Along with writing, another practice is to talk and really listen — to a family member or someone who could be your family. There are grandmas and grandpas all over this world who'd love to talk to you and share their stories! Ask them about times they remember. When was their first kiss? What was their favorite thing to do as a child?

Did they have a favorite toy? Did they know their grandparents? What was their favorite thing to eat? Where did they go to school? Ask with a sense of curiosity… you will be surprised at what you might hear. Have fun with it and keep practicing!

Life is too short for regret.

Radiant Reset Journaling

To unlock the power of your own story through journaling, below are a few prompts to begin. Give yourself the gift of exploring through writing freely, finding the true you to gain insights, to ignite (or re-ignite) your passion, and to transform your everyday life into one with meaning and purpose.

Find a comfortable journal, dedicate it to your SELF, and begin. Let yourself and your words flow. Write for your own soul, not for anyone else's eyes.

You might start with letters.

What would you honestly write to your 5-year-old self? What would you say to her at 10? 13? 30? As she aged? At the end of her life?

AMAZING WOMAN DIVINE LEGACY

Remember an incident, whether recent or past, that incited a strong reaction in you. It could've been hot passion, rage, sorrow, shame, joy, pride, exuberance; a strong emotion (or any of them). What circumstance, person, or incident brought up these strong emotions in you?

_____
_____
_____
_____
_____
_____
_____
_____
_____
_____
_____
_____
_____
_____

AMAZING WOMAN DIVINE LEGACY

What passionate feelings appear for you now? When? What triggers you?

___

AMAZING WOMAN DIVINE LEGACY

What other times in your life did you feel so impassioned? What similarities/differences do you find? Write from your gut.

AMAZING WOMAN DIVINE LEGACY

Write about stages in your life, capturing a timeline of sorts. Notice patterns that have recurred throughout your life. Those patterns are what created your stories.

AMAZING WOMAN DIVINE LEGACY

*You are worth coming home to yourself.
Every one of us is worth coming home to.*
~ Angaangaq

About Diane Sova

Diane Sova's mission in life is to create transformational awareness and connection between people, generations, cultures, and belief systems.

Diane is a respected author, historian, and accomplished editor. Known as "The Book Catalyst" and even referred to as a book savant, in addition to her editing services she hosts writing groups and circles, connecting people both to their inner worlds and to the outer world.

Her passion for celebrating people's legacies led her to create a book series, with the intention of inspiring curiosity about our world, our neighbors, and ourselves.

These stories change the way we view aging and the value of our ancestors' experiences. As an editor, she understands each writer's unique voice and approach, allowing their authenticity to shine through their stories. With passion,

Diane coaches the liberation of memories to share vision through the written word.

To broaden the beneficial impacts of storytelling and writing, she created programs to bring people together with the common intention of writing their own stories, accessing their passions and visions while weaving connections to their past and to each other. Elderly people in these programs who once felt forgotten have found themselves the center of attention, their tales of resilience and love inspiring those who had never taken time to listen before, adding a sense of being valued for their time on this earth.

Diane is devoted to bringing people to an awareness of their own divinity and sacredness. Called a "practical visionary" by friends, she has made several World Tours and travels often, making the study of multi-cultural healing, spiritual paths, cooperation and connection between people her life's work.

Her academic studies have spanned science and spirit. After earning her first degree in Business, she went on to earn her bachelor's degree in System Engineering, subsequently working 42 years in the aerospace industry. During those years, she continued her studies and earned undergraduate degrees in Cultural Anthropology, then Comparative Religion. Later, Diane went on to earn her master's degree in Space Operations and her master's degree in Religious Studies. These seemingly polar opposites actually enable her to readily bridge different cultures and beliefs. She has been recognized as a Global Citizen Ambassador by the U.S. State Department.

Diane is also a medium and strong channel of psychic energy. She has been deeply involved with sacred energy, healing, and shamanic practices through various spiritual pathways since the late 1970s, leading or participating in hundreds of ceremonies and spiritual initiations worldwide. She organizes and leads small, personalized group tours to special places of spiritual power. Diane is a writer, a published poet, a playwright (Letters to My Angels), an artist, a book editor, and a ceremonial leader.

To learn more about Diane Sova and her work, visit: www.globalspiritpublishing.com.

For editing or group inquiries email: diane@globalspiritpublishing.com.

Dedicated to the women who have felt rejected, hidden, or wounded by religion.

May you be free to seek a deeper connection with God and your spirituality.

It's your time to fall back in love with your own divinity, acknowledge the feminine face of God within, and embrace the beauty and the fullness of who you were always created to be.

Kristi Lynn Olson

Chapter 3

Finding the Feminine Face of God

Kristi Lynn Olson

*"She dares to greet challenges with the presence of love.
She remains open to gaining a higher level
of remembering her own wisdom.
And reclaims her inner divinity of God within.
This is the feminine face of God."*

As a young girl growing up in the Christian church, I loved hearing the stories of the bible. I especially loved how Esther became Queen after receiving a whole year of spa treatments, or how Mary Magdalene was healed from her demons and able to become part of Jesus' ministry. Ruth, the daughter-in-law of Naomi was able to find her perfect husband after becoming a widow just by listening to the advice of her mother-in-law. It all seemed like a beautiful fairytale. Until it wasn't.

As I grew up and began to examine ancient scriptures and historical writing for myself, I began to discern a new truth that not only perpetuated a system of patriarchy and viewed many women as prostitutes but, in many cases had entirely erased the presence of the feminine face of God. I believed there was so much more to these women than the stories that were told. There had to be a beauty and a lost wisdom from these women that would show me a reflection of the feminine face of God I felt was missing and awaken me to a deeper understanding of my own wisdom and connection to the divine.

What does the Feminine face of God look like?

My vision has always been to create a new view of theology for women who have felt rejected and hidden — a way of giving a voice and a face to the remembrance of their true essence. During my lifelong study of ancient scripture and spiritual wisdom, I have learned how to translate that ancient wisdom into practical application for today's woman who is seeking a deeper connection with God, with her spirituality, and with her own inner divinity, which is her divine feminine nature. I call that the feminine face of God.

In a time when she may feel, and even believe, that God has abandoned her or feel a disconnection from God and from her sense of self, she suffers in silence from a woundedness that prevents her from living her wholeness, her full essence.

*It is a time that we, as a collective,
must fall back in love with our own divinity,
acknowledge the feminine face of God within each of us
and embrace the fullness of who we
were always created to be.*

But what does she look like?

What does the presence of the divine within me, the feminine face of God look like?

What does she represent and how does she show up healed and whole through each of us?

I believe we are just waking up to a deeper understanding of the feminine face of God, who she is, and all she represents.

Many times, I have heard that she needs to have a certain skin color, be identified as a member of a certain culture, or speak a specific language. But from my perspective, she is not any of that. The feminine face of God is an essence. She has attributes that we can all relate to. When we get to know her, we will begin to understand how she shines through me and you in service to others.

> *Living in the state of Ruach means connecting deeply with the aspects of our divinity that reflect the feminine face of God as we express our own feminine wisdom, discernment, and unique essence to the world around us, using our gifts in service to others.*

The feminine face of God is multifaceted and multidimensional. She is an essence or a state of being. She is what I know to be living in Ruach. Ruach is a feminine noun in the Hebrew language, meaning spirit or breath, invisible force or power. It is also a word to express attributes such as intelligence, truth, hope, faith, knowledge, wisdom, discernment, infinity, and holiness, all reflecting the infinite power of the divine feminine.

Living in a state of Ruach restores,
revives, and allows us to remember our wisdom
and how deeply we are loved by God
as we allow the divine to
continually flow in and through us in love.

Ruach is the breath of God flowing through she who is open to receive and experience it. It is the intrinsic nature of the breath of God. Some cultures refer to it as Wind, Spirit, or Life. She is the essence of God, and as she lives in and flows through you, she is the essence of YOU. She dares to greet challenges with the presence of love and remains open to gaining a higher level of remembering her own wisdom and reclaiming her inner divinity of God within her. That is the feminine face of God.

When she heals from the many ways she's judged or
condemned herself, she gains the opportunity to become
a mirror of beauty, strength, and power. She moves
others to awaken to their divine feminine essence. She
naturally lives in a state of Ruach as a shining example
to others of the attributes of the feminine face of God.

As she heals from the many ways she's judged or condemned herself, she gains the opportunity to become a mirror of beauty, strength, and power. She becomes who she truly is and has always been. In doing so, she moves others to awaken to their divine feminine essence. She lives to be an example to others, living from a state of Ruach, as an example of the feminine face of God. Every physical face will look different, but the attributes and characteristics will shine through to represent a pure and lovely representation of the divine feminine essence of God.

Here are just some of the attributes, but not all, of the feminine face of God that you will notice in yourself and others once you start living in a continual state of Ruach:

1. Greater sense of purpose
2. Higher self-awareness
3. Boldly speaking your wisdom
4. Fulfilling, loving relationships
5. Spontaneous joy
6. Confidence
7. Courage to move forward even when it doesn't make sense
8. Wholeness in all areas of your life
9. Empowered self-image
10. Expanded intuition

As I learn to embrace the essence
of the feminine face of God,
get familiar with her attributes
and learn how to live in a continual state of Ruach,
the breath of God, the invisible power
of the divine within me,
I begin to break through the chains
of my own boundaries that have kept me
hidden or diminished from becoming
the highest version of myself.

The more divine love and light that can shine through me in service to others, the more I understand the true essence of my divinity. And the more I realize the presence of God within me. It's from this place that I'm living in Ruach, deeply connecting with my God-self. I'm seeing the Shekinah, or the glory of the divine presence of God in me at work, spreading love and light in the world as a sacred act. This is the divine feminine face of God. This is divine love that flows in and through me.

This is what we are awakening to as the truth…
the feminine face of God is a presence.
She is an essence.
She is Wind, Spirit, Life.

She is the intrinsic nature of the breath of God flowing through you and me if you are open to receiving and experiencing her in all her fullness. She is waiting for you as you seek a deeper connection with God and your inner divinity as you embrace the fullness of the divine feminine nature within you.

What prevents us from revealing the feminine face of God?

What keeps us from allowing her the freedom to be heard?

What stops us from allowing her essence to flow through us?

My own experiences included a lot of inner woundedness taking place over a lifetime. These wounds blocked the view of the essence of the feminine face of God. And diminished trust in myself to become the messenger of what I'm now here to share. Some of it included religious wounds that created a painful and controlled relationship with my personal authority.

By giving away my authority it meant I trusted someone else outside of myself more than I trusted myself to make decisions about my life.

I was conditioned and raised in a world where authority was always outside of me. I was never allowed to be in control of my own path or my own decisions. This pattern manifested into people pleasing and denying my own desires. By giving away my authority it meant I trusted someone else outside of myself more than I trusted myself to make decisions about my life. It wasn't that I didn't know what I wanted. It was more like I gradually allowed those who I perceived to be in authority over me to make the decisions for me because I knew it was the easier path. I didn't like confrontation, and I knew that by remaining silent I was protecting myself. Those behaviors kept me safe. Yet, at the same time, they did damage to my self-esteem and affected my relationships in ways that I didn't understand until years later.

Giving up my personal authority and allowing someone to have power over me extended not just into my family life but into my spiritual life, my work life, and my relationships, and manifested into a variety of pain points in varying degrees over time. It showed up sometimes as depression, low self-esteem, loss of personal identity, or diminished self-worth. There were many times I felt my voice was silenced. I often felt the pain of loneliness, social anxiety, fear of judgment, and fear of authority. I lacked self-trust and had trust issues in relationships while experiencing abuse and domestic violence. I felt disconnected from society, friends, and community. I'm sure there were more, but honestly, I was trying so hard to pretend everything was fine that I didn't even know what was real anymore. I lived in fight-or-flight mode most of my life, and that impacted my mental, emotional, and physical health.

> *The religious wounding I have experienced runs deep and caused pain to my soul that was unimaginable in a way that still hurts to this day.*

Experiences like mine are not uncommon. Your inner wounding may come from another source and yet the results are very likely the same.

Inner wounding like this can take place in a variety of ways.

- A comment or criticism from someone we respect can be taken to heart and have lasting effects on a young child that keeps them from taking risks later in life.
- A lack of affirmation or affection from a loved one can give us the message that we are unlovable.
- Being ignored or constantly overlooked can make us feel invisible, hidden, and unworthy.

If you think about it, I'm sure you can come up with your own examples of inner wounding and how it might still show up in areas of your life today, no matter how big or small the wound may be. And here's what happens when that wound remains open and unhealed:

- We continue to experience the wound
- We feel the pain and suffering
- At some point, we stop loving ourselves
- We feel disconnected from the truth
- We feel abandoned
- We stop seeing the divine in ourselves

In essence, we no longer recognize the feminine face of God. We believe ourselves to be so wounded that we no longer feel safe, so why would we risk allowing her (the voice of our feminine face of God) the freedom to be heard again? We unknowingly perpetuate our own old stories of woundedness because it's comfortable to stay in the safety of the chaos rather than risk the fear of the unknown.

Most of all, we give up on ourselves because choosing to take back our power seems selfish at this point, if not unachievable. We believe the stories we tell ourselves. That we will never be good enough, we will never do it right, and we will never be able to show up again because of all the shame and guilt we have taken on. We convince ourselves that it must be our fault, and remaining hidden seems like the path of least resistance. Being happy doesn't matter anymore. Our only goal now is survival.

Perhaps the greatest pain caused by my own religious wounding can be witnessed in what I was willing to settle for in my personal relationships… clouded with abuse, domestic violence, and my inability to love myself. Honestly, I don't think I even knew what love looked like, let alone how to give or receive love.

I recently came to understand that I didn't have an accurate example of what love looked like as a child growing up, and the pain and misconception of that love carried a thread of dysfunction throughout my entire life. There is still some level of dysfunction to this day. As I am writing this, I only have a snapshot of what love looks like as I navigate these new revelations. All I know right now is that love set me up for confusion, and perhaps I learned to deny my feelings and deny my voice when it came to relationships. I also had feelings of not being enough and being too much at the same time. Unraveling and deconstructing those beliefs has been an integral part of my own healing journey.

The misconception of love brings with it the dysfunctional friends of guilt, shame, abandonment, and rejection. Those misconceptions of love became part of my identity. Unraveling and deconstructing those beliefs has been an integral part of my own healing journey.

When I experienced woundedness from the outside, I had to learn to heal from the inside out. It was only then that I could experience what I call the breath of expansion. It's like Ruach, the breath that moves through everything. The life force, or breath of life moving through me once again.

As I began to reacquaint myself with the attributes of the feminine face of God and remember who I always was, I realized that I was free to create a new story for myself. I was able to begin to breathe again. The relationship I could now rebuild with my inner divinity, restored, revived, and allowed me to remember my innate wisdom and how deeply I was loved by God. I reconnected to my sense of self. I allowed the feminine face of God to flow in and through me once again.

> *In healing my life from the inside out,*
> *once the inside began to heal,*
> *the outside changed to reflect my*
> *inner beauty and spiritual light.*
> *I can't explain it,*
> *but I looked different*
> *when I saw myself in the mirror.*

My friends said I looked different and kept asking me if I changed my hair or makeup. It wasn't a physical change. It was a spiritual change that reflected the love I now felt for myself… a love that came from deep within. My soul was going through a spiritual growth and that held much personal value for me.

I believe that my life story, as does yours, spans further than I can even imagine into eternity. It's about more than my future or purpose. It's about attaining growth and divine success without getting stuck in old patterns that no longer serve me. The healing process from the inside out sets in motion a call for spiritual assistance to help me meet any challenges that I may encounter so that my personal spiritual success can bring good to the world around me. I am here to serve with my gifts as a form of love. This is my new definition of love.

*I am blessed with extraordinary grace and
divine intervention when I need it.
I finally feel the complete love of the feminine face
of God. To continue to grow on my spiritual path to
soul consciousness, I'm continually called to heal
and release the pain held
in the undiscovered regions of my inner wounds.
I truly believe this will break the generational
wounds, steeped in beliefs of not being enough
and being too much at the same time.
I must acknowledge, forgive, release, and move forward.
This is how I move forward in love.*

This past fall I was fortunate enough to go on a very healing journey to the south of France with a good friend as we retraced the sacred steps of Mary Magdalene. We went to a river near Rennes-les-Bains where Mary Magdalene was said to have baptized followers of Jesus. I have always believed that there is a cleansing that takes place in a baptism, as well as a healing. So here… in the river where water cleanses, heals, and washes away the pain so light and love can enter… I asked my new friend John, who was leading us on the journey, to baptize me. The significance of the ritual of baptism at this sacred river does not escape me. Not only was it cleansing and healing for me on a spiritual level, but it was also healing to have John baptize me to signify my healing from abusive men in my past. John created a safe space for me. He'd shown me a kindness that can only come from a heart that has also known pain. He was now offering the gift of unconditional love, light, and freedom to me as I washed away my own pain from the past.

This is a memory I will always treasure deep in my heart. It was not a coincidence that I found a stone in the river there in the shape of a heart. I carried the stone home with me as a remembrance of this sacred place and time.

> *I am reminded to see the*
> *feminine face of God in myself and others,*
> *that she will bring angels of peace*
> *and is always there to guide me even if I don't see it.*
> *She speaks through my heart.*
> *That is where my inner wisdom is.*

If I ever feel alone, in stressful situations, or not heard by others, I am reminded that my inner wisdom, the feminine face of God within me, hears me, knows me, and loves me deeply. All I need to do is reach out and ask her to help me so that I can receive the comfort, connection, and support that I need for any given situation. I now know that I am worthy of this support from the divine, and I shouldn't hide or isolate myself, which only prevents me from receiving all the love that I need. In the past, that is what I would have done. I would have tried to figure it out myself and not ask for any help because that would show a sign of weakness. I thought that I had to be always seen as strong. I couldn't afford to let my guard down. Now I know that I can trust myself, the divine within and that I am safe with her.

I see my work as sacred.
And no matter what is happening in my life
I know that as I learn to embrace
my own inner divinity,
my divine feminine nature.
I am always being guided towards my heart,
which is my sacred inner temple.

This is where my inner wisdom resides, and I can trust her. It's as if I have been initiated into the power of my own heart. As I grow spiritually and heal from the inside out, the field of my heart grows, and my energetic influence becomes more important and impactful in using my gifts to heal the world around me through the work I do. I even feel that when I travel to different countries, at any given time I meet people who can feel the love and light of the feminine face of God flowing in and through me. Even if it's just a smile or a brief conversation, it makes a difference in how they feel validated and loved in just that single moment.

I trust that through this healing journey
of reclaiming my divine feminine nature,
my heart is enlarging with a love I don't yet understand.
And at the same time, it is healing the
world around me as others are touched by the
essence and love of the divine just by my presence.

I am blessed and humbled that even with the chaos of my past, I can still be of service in love to represent the fullness of the divine.

*If God reveals himself to us through his creation,
and we are his creation,
then "Christ lives in us, the hope of Glory."
(Colossians 1:27)
and we also represent the fullness of the divine.*

We are the feminine face of God as women who chose to reclaim our power and remember who we always were. We are of the lineage of the ancient ones who have the wisdom to heal and be healed.

By embracing this change and operating in your full essence, you are a powerful wind now able to bring change, justice, truth, wisdom, hope, healing, and peace to your life and to others. Your life breath matters.

Radiant Reset Journaling

On the following pages, you'll find journaling prompts.

Each question is designed to reveal an ever-evolving feminine face of God within you.

It is my intention to inspire you to explore your own relationship with 'her' in ways that will elevate your life.

If you have experienced any inner wounds or religious wounds in your life, what things have you kept hidden or diminished that may have kept you from becoming the highest version of yourself?

_____
_____
_____
_____
_____
_____
_____
_____
_____
_____
_____
_____
_____
_____

Kristi Lynn Olson

As you heal the wounds and begin to see yourself as worthy and a woman who carries the creative light of the divine within you, are you living the life you desire?

What more would you ask for?

Describe the life you truly desire to live in detail, and list one small shift you are ready to make to get closer to that life.

_____
_____
_____
_____
_____
_____
_____
_____
_____
_____
_____

Lack of self-worth can get in the way of asking for the help you need. Living in a state of Ruach doesn't make you more holy, but it does allow you the freedom to ask Spirit for more of what you need to be healed in ways you can't even imagine.

Sit quietly with your journal and invite the essence of God to flow through you.

Ask her for what you need in your healing journey and be open to receiving all that is meant for you.

_____
_____
_____
_____
_____
_____
_____
_____
_____
_____
_____

When you embrace your unique expression of the feminine face of God, you become part of a divine story. You begin to write the narrative of your own story as you learn to trust what feels right. You learn to use your gifts as you serve in love. You trust yourself to say yes to opportunities even if it doesn't make sense or you don't have all the details yet. Your divine feminine infinite power and wisdom allow you to birth new and creative ideas.

What is one idea that keeps coming up for you that you are ready to say YES to?

_____
_____
_____
_____
_____
_____
_____
_____
_____
_____

Kristi Lynn Olson

As you begin to reconnect to your inner divinity and allow the feminine face of God to flow in and through you, what attributes do you want to reawaken within yourself as a representation of the divine feminine essence of God within?

_____
_____
_____
_____
_____
_____
_____
_____
_____
_____
_____
_____
_____
_____
_____
_____
_____

About Kristi Lynn Olson

"In a time when so many women are feeling silenced, rejected, and hidden, I feel it is essential that we redefine our view of theology for women and create spiritual practices that lead us into a deeper connection with God. We need to fall back in love with our own divinity and acknowledge the feminine face of God within us as we embrace the beauty of our true essence. By combining ancient scripture and sacred wisdom, we can begin to heal the inner wounds that have kept women's voices silent and, as a collective, revive a renewed sense of spiritual identity and wholeness."

Kristi Lynn Olson calls herself a Transitional Theologian. She is a woman of a new era who is merging religion and spirituality. She is a scholar of ancient religion, a woman who had an awakening of her own inner divinity. This took her on a quest to find the feminine face of God, which she believes has been hidden or erased from history.

She is a master teacher, healer, and spiritual guide for women. Many people have said she is an alchemist of healing religious trauma and has often been called a spiritual heart surgeon. She sees her work as a sacred blending of the unique ability to translate ancient wisdom into practical application for today's woman seeking a deeper connection with God and her own inner divinity, her divine feminine nature, and those aspects of her that have been rejected, denied, or diminished due to Religious Wounding and Trauma.

> *Kristi Lynn Olson is gifted with the ability to merge religion with spirituality, engaging both the lineage of sacred healing and the wisdom of ancient scripture.*
> *She believes that with a rich and in-depth understanding of ancient scripture and sacred wisdom, she can take women into a new era of divine feminine consciousness, as they seek to understand what the feminine face of God looks like and how it relates to them as women searching for a renewed sense of spiritual identity and wholeness.*

It is her vision to create a new view of theology for women who have felt rejected and hidden… giving voice to the remembrance of their true essence. Through master classes, Soul Realignment work, and one-on-one personal mentoring, Kristi uses her natural gifts as a seer, healer, and spiritual guide to help women do the deep inner healing work to awaken a remembering of their own unique essence of their inner divinity.

To learn more about Kristi Lynn Olson and her work visit:
www.KristiLynnOlson.com

Dedicated to those who are
awakening the Artistry of Alchemy…
to the artists rising to live life with inspiration…
walking a path of embodied authentic intuition…
embracing the creative heart center and
the courage to pause and listen.
The time is now.

CeCe Sanchez

Chapter 4

Awaken the Artistry of Alchemy

CeCe Sanchez

*The way of the alchemist
symbolizes creative transformation
through the growth of authentic expression.
She successfully expresses herself through Love.
She honors the power of quietude over the
noise and chaos of a distracted mind.
She knows her power and freely expresses it.*

Why is it so easy for me to answer the calling of my authentic self?

This is the question I asked myself, and what I discovered amazed me.

I am passionate about sharing my years of training…

Travels to Thailand and the study of Thai Massage.

Magical experiences in New Zealand, exploring the power of healing with hot white stones amplifying dreams and visions, and connecting with spirit guides and the feminine energies of the cosmic stars.

Diving into the energy of Chi Gong taught by a Master Teacher.

Reiki. Acupressure. Study of Tui Nu That supports the body's own healing process.

My time in Japan was spent studying Belly dancing, hatha yoga, levitating meditation and walking on hot coals. Mind over matter experiences

Experiencing laughter yoga with the creator and laughing for no reason increases breathing and lowers stress and has positive effects on wellbeing.

And so much more.

The fascination of being in my body and the ancient wisdom of people seeking to know the body and healing of the body became my passion.

Today, I see these experiences brought me to an awakening of my own feeling body. And learning ways to truly own my authentic expression. And find my purpose in art.

*It is time to set free
and have the courage to live your creative life.
Live each moment to the fullest
and embrace your creativity.*

*Being an artist and
staying true to our authentic selves is
a decision that comes from within.
We are creative souls on a journey,*

and pursuing our dreams is essential.
Take one step today toward your dream,
no matter how small.

It's time to bring all the pieces of your abandoned self together and follow your inspiration.

As a child, I was innately guided to healing through the power of nature. My first memories are of my two-year-old self wandering across a country highway road… to the creek and deep into the full-bloomed mustard field… immersing myself in a sea of 3-foot-tall chartreuse stems and bright yellow blooms. Maybe it was the color that drew me in. Or maybe it was my innate knowledge of the medicinal qualities of the energy of this plant? Maybe it came from a prior lifetime? Or from the earth herself. I truly do not know.

But the heart of the healer was embraced. This became my purposeful path.

Nature is infinitely creative.
It always produces the possibility of new beginnings.
—Marianne Williamson

Are you ready to transform your life?

Embarking on a journey of self-discovery can unlock your true potential, freeing your creativity and empowering you to live a life that reflects your core values and beliefs.

CeCe Sanchez

I found a passion that flourished in the exploration of my version of what it would mean to be impassioned by the transformational art of healing.

Vivid imagination became the palette of creating my world. It was not always easy; I was raised in the 70s as a latchkey kid by a single mom, living from day-to-day, sometimes on food stamps. No, life wasn't always easy. But there were things where I quickly found a respite away from the concerns. Art and creativity were my favorite pastimes, as were spending hours cutting out magazines and creating a vision board.

These experiences with art and creativity helped me overcome my challenges as a latchkey kid.

Being immersed in the feeling body, like putting on a record player, dancing with my sister, and giggling about the songs we would dance to. Or the richness of long, hot summer days, buttery cake batter, juicy watermelon, sweet/sour lemonade made from our own lemon bush, and add of a spoonful of sugar, and the neighbor's pool, Kool-aide, and pizza. Reflecting on my childhood shaped my views on creativity and resilience.

During the hot summer nights, we used to sleep outside under the blanket of stars and the moon. During the day, we would put on circus shows and performances with the kids in our neighborhood. We had plenty of time and freedom to do what we wanted until the streetlights turned on unless it was a nighttime hide-and-seek game. It was always wild and fun.

As the season shifted into autumn, we enjoyed the changing colors of the leaves that fell like a blaze of crimson, gold, and orange hues. We rake the leaves into intricate patterns, creating embellished labyrinths, spirals, and magical trails. Every step on the morning dew grass was a crunch underfoot, bringing the smell of earth and fresh falling leaves closer to something exciting and unknown.

We would recycle our old gifts, hide them in treasure hunts, and relish the joy of discovery and play. These moments of imagination and discovery were priceless. During these moments, we found significant expansion in our discovery of play. I remember being fearless while riding my horse to the river after a pouring winter rain and swimming with her. I had pure trust in my strength, body wisdom, and total respect for my horse, Sharon. She allowed me to hang on to her tail as she swam. These were the moments I cherished the most.

> *Creativity is a powerful tool that guides*
> *And supports us through tough times.*
> *By observing and witnessing ourselves,*
> *we can start a journey of living*
> *an active, creative life.*

Creativity is supported by embodiment practices such as awareness, movement, breath, and sound. These are avenues to body wisdom and inspiring creativity.

As an alchemist, you know that resetting your dreams with daily gratitude and reflection before bed is essential.

Imagine waking up feeling refreshed, energized, and focused.

Art flow supports your inner wisdom.
Listen to your heart.
It will guide you and serve as your
muse, mentor, and mastermind.
The transformation begins when we embrace our creativity
and start setting up space for it, one day at a time.
In the meantime, we can use a pen and notebook to
doodle, dream, and clear our minds.

You start your day by tuning your mind and body as an instrument to harmonize perfectly with your creative surroundings. Gratitude lets you connect with your inner wisdom, guiding you throughout the day. With a clear mind and a grounded heart, you are free to move forward with purpose and direction. By unlocking your potential with embodiment practices you are empowered to release emotional blockages and awaken your mind, body, and spirit and shed light on the shadow.

Affirmations can support our subconscious.
Nature can inspire our soul, and embodied movements
such as walking, yoga, dancing and
sounding can uplift our spirits."

These Practices Lead to Body Wisdom and Inspire Creativity

There are many activities to choose from, like yoga, dance, mindfulness, and breathing exercises that help connect the mind and body.

- Meditation and moving meditations support clearing the mind and calming the body.
- Taking walks in and around nature, practicing yoga movements or dance, and creating art or writing all help release stress, support cognition, and ground the body-mind.
- Nurture your creative nature. Practicing embodiment routines can help us feel clarity, more alive, and free.

These embodiment practices can lead to discovering more about oneself, healing, and personal growth. Our natural intuition has a lot of power and can guide us to heal. We all possess an innate ability to be creative and are inherently attracted to nature's immense power. By spending time in nature, we can tap into its healing power and find what we need to heal.

What inspires us to create?
What is the difference between inspiration and intuition?
What motivates you to create?

We are inspired by what we see, a certain someone, or a muse. We could find it by being around other artists or free writing in our journals. It begins by trusting your intuition and bravely allowing yourself to try new things.

Here are a few tools to help you to change up your routine and begin to see the world differently:

- Write with the other hand in your journal.
- Ask yourself what you are avoiding.
- Listen into the space often called the shadow, the space that's scared and is trying to protect you.

> *The way of Artistry of Alchemy*
> *is a path that allows us to explore*
> *our creativity and the inner world.*
> *This journey is about self-discovery, empowerment,*
> *and living a consciously brave,*
> *fulfilling, inspiring, and creative life.*

The alchemist's journey, from frustration to inspiration, highlights the transformative power of adopting a mindset focused on creative liberation. The alchemist's practice recognizes the value of play, messy experimentation, and exploration in cultivating an environment that fosters creativity.

> *The urge to express and live a more inspired life,*
> *shifted in 2020 into a state of opportunities,*
> *forcing me to ask myself,*
> *"If not now, when?"*
> *I suddenly overcame my fear of*
> *making mistakes and striving for perfection.*
> *No more excuses.*

As a young woman, I was drawn to becoming certified in body-centric practices. The world of yoga, dance, breathwork, meditation, and hands-on healing moved well beyond a hobby. It became the foundation of my trailblazing commitment to creatively expressing through the sacred arts and work in the field of somatic practices, and the body became a canvas.

My intuition was calling me into why I was here.

It is easy because it is who I am.

I am led by spirit.

My feeling body intelligence calms when I open to my authentic wisdom self.

The knowledge of innate wisdom moves me in this direction of being.

I see life in pictures.

I connect the dots.

Color expresses life through me, and like a lotus, I open.

My spirit shines.

Ease of life begins to flow.

The path is clear to create. I land in deepened trust.

It is easy for me to answer my calling.

It is the right thing to do:
Be authentic, creative, healing,
and calming to the nervous system.

Let us awaken our passions and creativity.

To design your life…
to see your authentic power…
to embrace transformation…
This is becoming an artist of alchemy.
And I know this to be the path of unbridled creativity.

The way of the creative alchemist symbolizes insight, transformation, and intelligence. It is success expressed in love. It honors the power of quietude while sifting through the rambling noise or an unsettled, agitated, distracted mind. And a realization of the creative essence accessed through embodied practices that inspire stillness within movement.

Understanding your power gives you way
to take action on your quest.
Be unapologetic.
Rise with it, and don't dim your light.
This is your life to shine.
You are unique. You are a miracle!
Find and explore what delights you and go for it.
Through the creative process,
you will give yourself time and space.

What is whimsical and magical to you?
How can you surround yourself with this beauty?

Authentic, unbridled creativity symbolizes an inner environment that flourishes in confidence. Acceptance of all of it… awareness of all distractions… those things that steal your attention away from the callings of your heart… the source of your creativity.

Don't look outside yourself. Drop into the heart.
Let go of the how. Allow life to reveal its gifts.
It is the beauty of noticing.
It is the power of transforming doubt into love.
Happiness always comes from listening to your heart
and embracing the artistry of alchemy.

Love all your path of creation… Let yourself be supported and strong.

Allow the past to give you strength. Lean into the present moment.

The past cannot be changed.

But the past can become the creative wisdom to inform an empowered future.

> *"The creative act is not hanging on,*
> *but yielding to a new creative movement.*
> *Awe is what moves us forward."*
> —*Joseph Campbell*

Find the freedom of realizing all you have experienced and all you have come through as wisdom teachings designed to bring you to this moment and guiding you to where you desire to go.

*Are you willing to speak gently to your inner artist
and give encouraging words?
Or do you need a booming loudspeaker
to remember your magnificence?*

This is you, A bright source of creative flow!

*Are you willing to love, look into your eyes, and say
I love you... I know I am a spiritual, intelligent,
radiant source of creative love?*

When we realize our unique, authentic self as nature, we stay true, and the power of self-direction is revealed. Every moment is a new beginning; find wonderment in the beauty of nature.

- *Could nature be the answer for inspiration?*
- *Are you living in the infinite power of now?*
- *Are you aware that you are nature?*
- *How will knowing that you are a part of nature shift you to create?*

*Keep on keeping on.
Say Yes to your dreams and visions; you got this.
Keep on keeping on with creativity and manifesting
your life because you say so.
I believe in my art and soul, so I am moving forward.*

Commit to begin by:

- Access the power of your emotions so they fuel you rather than paralyze you.
- Allow your creative potential to speak to you through journaling.
- Explore what sparks joy.
- Deepen the awakening of your body through embodied practices that support your creative flow.
- Live in inspiration.
- Devote yourself to increasing self-esteem, self-love, and self-care.
- Revel in newfound courage and clarity, gain confidence through movement, and promote well-being.
- Rekindle your creative birthright.
- Be Brave!

In the words of Georgia O'Keefe:

> *"To create one's world in any of the arts takes courage.*
> *I decided to start anew,*
> *to strip away what I had been taught.*
> *I decided that if I could paint that flower on a huge scale,*
> *you could not ignore its beauty.*
> *The days you work are the best."*

After reading her words, I realized that courage is simply the act of loving oneself.

So, I ask you:

- *Are you ready to stand up for your heart and passions and pursue a life as a creative?*
- *Are you willing to give it your all and live with wonder and amazement?*
- *What does that life look like for you?*
- *Will you act towards achieving it today?*

> *When we move toward our creativity, we move toward our Creator. We find ourselves becoming more creative when we seek to become more spiritual. Our creativity and spirituality are so closely interconnected that they are, in effect, the same thing.*
> —Deepak Chopra

Art making feels like time standing still, and I am neither past nor future; I am in the infinite now. When I feel the creator spirit move me and it all aligns, I feel so divinely connected to the power of innate wisdom, an intelligence of world mysteries.

What have you moved towards that was creatively divine?

Do you feel that your creativity is spiritual? If so, what is an example?

When did you feel closely interconnected through writing or painting?

Embracing my iconic power has changed how I see things.
It has impacted me in ways that I had only dreamt of.
Now, I know I am not dreaming.
Because I am living the dream.

I now know that iconic power is to be the artist of my own life. This one mere simple acknowledgment opens my heart and soul's work. Once I experienced this kind of authentic flow, I knew true courage. This courage gives me the focus and energy to fulfill my dreams.

Art: It's our connection to the world…
our innate language that carries the power to
express our iconic human experience.

Becoming an Artistry of Alchemy teaches us ways to:

- Honor our own creative wisdom.
- Dissolve creative blocks.
- Lift the ceiling of one's thinking.
- Access authentic expression.
- Ignite natural motivation.
- Empower a commitment to live into the capacities of your inner creative artist.
- Make healthy and wise choices.
- Allow a natural curiosity to open a playful spirit.
- Embrace new potentials and allow them to be realized.

We can access our artistic alchemist power by asking questions that ignite the heart and soul of our creative destiny.

Creativity is inspired by daily practice. That's why the first dedicated step is to create a space that's your own. It's like a lifeline to committing to action, allowing yourself the time and space to be creative radiance. It's time to get prepared. Clear out the old and allow in the new.

I once read about a woman who lived in an eight-by-eleven room in New York City. Even in the smallest living spaces, she anchored in an experience to create with a small wooden table and a meditation pillow she picked up at a second-hand store. Another example is that of acclaimed mythologist Joseph Campbell, who I once read traveled with a 'special' ink pen and journal that marks his sacred creative space. The point is your space is your space… regardless of the size… or… *Imagine now where you can create a space.*

A space where you can use your imagination often.
Value your creativity.
Give yourself permission to dream.

It was Yayoi Kusama who said: *"A polka-dot has the form of the sun, which is a symbol of the energy of the whole world and our living life, and also the form of the moon, which is calm."*

For me, this artist stands for individuality. Her power is her uniqueness. A dot says it all. Imagine finding your passion in a dot. And this leads to tremendous passion in your life. It is time to connect the dots…

I encourage you to follow suit and be inspired. Doodle with dots. Are you ready to *'dot it out'*? Just do it! Imagine all the dots like a treasure map that will fuel your soul and passions. Create your own universe.

Allow yourself the intimacy, time, and space to acknowledge all you truly desire to create with a willingness to know what no longer supports. That's why the second dedicated step is a commitment to clear boundaries and making the space for your creative imagination to soar!

What are three things that distract you from creating?

> *"You Can't Use Up Creativity,*
> *the More You Use the More You Have."*
> —Maya Angelou

Making a commitment to your creativity opens the heart to your soul.

What if your creativity is your gift back to the universe?

Can you imagine all you could create if you kept going?

How could being more curious fuel your creativity?

Your creativity is your unique signature. What if your spark ignites a positive change in the world?

Declare: Yes. Yes Universe. Give yourself a sense of direction.

Consider, what is ONE ACTION you can take right now that will lead you to that which you most desire to create?

*Don't wait any longer.
Allow yourself to experience the
breakthroughs you've longed for.
Remember, creativity is food for the soul.*

Authenticity is the doorway to higher creativity and an expansive, creative future. As you envision your life as an Artist of Alchemy, consider ways to actualize your own authentic expression. The key is consistency and dedication in establishing a practice to amplify a more productive and embodied creative life where art meets spirituality meets transformation. This is the way we can become more embodied, connected to the core of our natural creative beings, and find direction in our intuition. Map out your vision. Utilize play of the imagination.

We can move through obstacles on our path to self-growth and cultivate self-love: By remembering that everything is energy, even our thoughts… and by stimulating the senses, nature supports a profound connection and strengthens the creative soul. Here we find ways that refreshes, inspires, and offers vast beauty, serenity, and healing qualities.

> "Art is standing with one hand extended into the universe
> and one hand extended into the world,
> and letting ourselves be a conduit for passing energy."
> —Albert Einstein

Begin now: Commit to become an artist of alchemy. The path of an Artist of Alchemy is one paved in authentic creative power. Reclaim your creativity and relationship to time and space. Taking the time to slow down. Shifting and creating a container to set boundaries, get back in touch. Take time to look deep, discern the shadow self, and work with all aspects of self.

Most of all, remember:

This is about loving all of you. You are worthy of it all.

Radiant Reset Journaling

The power to create your life is here now. You are ready to begin again. Are you ready to transform your life? Is it time to immerse into your feeling body? This awareness of yes is the grounding force leading you from the heart. Relaxing into this space of allowing is limitless flow it responds to our higher souls' purpose, and it holds the voice of our intuition.

On the following pages you'll find journaling prompts.

Each question is designed to awaken the artist of alchemy within you... rising to live life with inspiration... walking a path of embodied authentic intuition... embracing the creative heart center and, the courage to pause and listen.

Pause: before we write, I invite you to put on deep, downtempo, earthy tones, slow vocal sounds, lush electronic music, drums, or extended, slow tones-didgeridoo mix. The kind of music that inspires you to feel the sensation of the body. I invite you to lie down comfortably and connect to the earth. Let your body gently rock, stretch, and roll slowly to one side and the other like an amoeba. Breathe into your whole body. Pulse and feel. Feel the sensation of the water body down to the cellular level and the connection to the grounding force of gravity. These moves will help you let go. Continue to breathe and sound out if it feels comfortable. Do this for 5 to 10 minutes or as long as you like. And when you feel ready journal.

Creative Liberation

Are you willing to shift and take the first step to reclaim your creativity?

Are you ready to sense more clarity and feel aliveness and flow?

How will making these changes impact your life and your future?

_____

_____

_____

_____

_____

_____

_____

_____

_____

AMAZING WOMAN DIVINE LEGACY

Coming Home Creative Soul Journey

What gifts do you have or would like to discover or creatively nurture?

_____
_____
_____
_____
_____
_____
_____
_____
_____
_____
_____
_____
_____
_____

AMAZING WOMAN DIVINE LEGACY

Innate Wisdom:
Sensations of Life Force Energy

Do you trust your intuition to navigate you?

Have you ever listened to your body's sensations to guide you, and what did you discover?

_____
_____
_____
_____
_____
_____
_____
_____
_____
_____
_____

AMAZING WOMAN DIVINE LEGACY

Self-Expression: Soul's True Purpose

Move from resistance into flow, Give yourself permission to dream, shine your unique self, and feel your soul. What do you desire? What commitment would you take as the 1st action step towards living your creative radiance? What does it look like?

_____

_____

_____

_____

_____

_____

_____

_____

_____

_____

_____

_____

AMAZING WOMAN DIVINE LEGACY

Heart and Soul of Creative Destiny

This is an invitation for intimacy with time and space. Allow the body to get excited. See yourself anchored in Creative Radiance and aligned with your Divine Soul's purpose.

Are you ready to transform your life? It is time to feel into your feeling body. You are living creatively expressed; how will you let your playful spirit out while you create space for the awakening?

AMAZING WOMAN DIVINE LEGACY

About CeCe Sanchez

CeCe is the creator of the Artistry of Alchemy, an expressive collection of transformational embodied practices. For over three decades, she has supported individuals' emotional processes through art, mindfulness, journaling, and meditation. An impassioned teacher she nurtures community and intentional creativity through Artistry of Alchemy transformational journeys and retreats that include embodied transformational dance, circles, and art creation.

Her approach to healing through art and intentional creativity is empowering, and CeCe seeks to elevate, awaken, and support the authentic self by accessing higher creativity.

She believes that creativity is a birthright and our natural way of expressing ourselves, and it matters because it is how we give back our gifts to the world. Creativity inspires new ways of seeing and helps one to be more alive, motivated, and fulfilled. CeCe's work encourages play and self-discovery to recover one's natural, authentic self in tune with nature and provides a space to fall in love with oneself. It is CeCe's philosophy that when we are in love, we can heal and see others as we all belong.

The Artistry of Alchemy is inspirational and supports navigating the creative heart.

To learn more about CeCe Sanchez and her work visit:
www.CeCeSanchez.com
Or follow her on Instagram @CeCe Spirit

Dedicated to women around the world who are feeling that inner prompting and knowing there is something more.

May the spark of your soul radiantly shine as you step into your worthiness, deep inner joy, recognizing your worth and value.

Becky Norwood

Chapter 5

Does Your Soul Shine?

Becky Norwood

*It is better to walk in light than to dance in darkness.
The inner light shines from love, compassion, and faith.
If there is light in your heart,
there can be no darkness in your soul.*

Often, our world today can feel tumultuous and disconcerting. And yet, in spite and despite all of the unrest, there is one thing we DO have the ability to control... and that is ourselves.

As I re-read this chapter... what I wrote a year ago... still holds true. But it is quite amazing that I can see my own growth. It is not that certain less-than-stellar situations have changed. I find that with my willingness to explore letting my light shine, I am responding rather than reacting, and there is a big difference between the two.

Does it mean that I no longer experience grief and sadness? No, in fact, in full disclosure there have been times when I felt anger and despair. Yet, I find myself acknowledging the feelings and responding differently than I have in the past. Maybe it is with resignation for the things I have no idea how to change, acceptance, and the spark that keeps living with in me. That spark to radiate joyfulness, gratitude, wholeness and peacefulness.

> *When we put pen to paper with the intention of sharing the stories of our life's journey with the world, we come to understand that there is a certain magic that happens.*

Our written words will hopefully land just right for someone who is likewise struggling with something that is so profound, so heart wrenching… that it is difficult to see the light. Maybe it is just one person who will read our words and be comforted and also inspired to take a closer look at their own life with a new perspective on their own circumstance. Maybe it will reach and start a spark for many ready to live into their radiant legacy. We cannot control who will read our words and rejoice… but we can be mindful of our own quest to let our own soul shine.

When we release our words whether they are in the pages of a book, from the stage, or just to our closest of friends it often leads to transformation.

I can see the contrast of what a year has brought to my life. Seeing that contrast has enlightened my heart to see that I have grown over this past year. We seldom see it in the day-to-day. But we do see it when we look back and even, as is the case here… realize there is growth, there is acceptance, and that I have dug way deeper into other aspects of myself than I had realized. The power is in the contrast.

I am quite sure that not one of us has NOT gone through truly rough times. The times that are often considered the dark night of the soul. Yet through these dark, soul-wrenching experiences, a spark inside us becomes a glowing ember and an inner flame. A flame unwilling to be snuffed out. I fully realize that I do not hold a corner on the market for tough things I have suffered with, coped with, learned from, and cried over. There is always someone dealing with far worse.

*The question is, are we willing to grow
and change and yes, thrive.
Do we look at ourselves
and ask one very important question:
Who am I afraid to disappoint?*

Perhaps we are not really in fear of disappointing someone else. Perhaps we are in fear of disappointing ourselves! And it is in facing that fear, acknowledging it, that the fear dissolves, and we begin to see and sense our worthiness.

We may even experience anger. But facing it, acknowledging it, and releasing it, is where growth happens.

Growing up, I was at the mercy of a highly abusive father. He was a Jekel and Hyde — multiple personality type person who could and did charm the socks off of anyone he came in contact with. As a child, we first were Lutheran, then he insisted we become Rosicrucian, then Jehovah's Witness, then Catholic, then Mormon. And every time, he would advance quickly up to positions of responsibility... until people disappointed him (or quite possibly they caught on to his abusive tendencies). Either way, we would be instructed to ride along — forsake all friendships and move on to the next BEST thing.

There were many instances where a tragedy in the U.S. (suspicious things like train derailments and the Oklahoma bombings). would prompt an investigative visit from the FBI, due to his radical hate-filled reproach of U.S. politics.

Combine that with the constant reminder of being ugly, stupid, and worth NOTHING, which was the mantra that he ranted constantly, not just to me but to my siblings and even my mother — and you get a family that was in a state of confusion at all times. Mental, physical, emotional, and sexual abuse was the norm. The little girl in me lost the magic of make-believe and joy around four years old, and it took me well into adulthood to awaken the recognition of the goodness within me.

As the oldest daughter, I was responsible for my siblings. I was put in charge of making sure they were doing what they were supposed to do. Fail at that — even at eight years old, and it meant not only watching them get beat senseless, but it also meant the same for me, and often worse. His children were his slaves, in many more ways than one. Play was seldom allowed. We were alienated from all our extended family. He moved us far away from them and allowed no contact. Entering the teen years, as he sensed the slightest sense of rebellion, there was the incessant threat that he knew how to end our lives.

*It was not that there was not a spark left inside me.
It was that I did not know how to access it.
I felt enslaved and in deep, raw fear for my life.*

As happens to likely most women who grow up in such an environment, we do not have a healthy barometer of what is healthy and normal… we grew up in an abnormally unhealthy environment. So as we enter adulthood we see life through a dysfunctional lens and go on to attract the same into our life.

My first marriage was no exception. I married a man much like my father, but my awareness… that deep inner yearning and knowingness that there has to be something better… was creating a restlessness within my soul. I was no longer willing to listen to the *'shit talk'*, the undermining of worthiness, the constant beratement, and the threats.

That marriage lasted less than three years — providing me with two beautiful daughters. I was six months pregnant with my second baby and the oldest was thirteen months old when I entered single-parenthood and went on to raise them completely on my own — without support. He chose not to be a part of their lives.

In the meantime, my father chose to take his life, unable to deal with the guilt of his horrible behavior.

I chose not to get involved in another relationship until my daughters were grown. I was too afraid I would attract the same into my life.

The road was tough for a while, but those years of raising my daughters alone afforded me the freedom to explore what happiness looked like. I explored many religions; I explored many forms of what was then considered New Age. I read voraciously, spent time in nature, and spent lots of time with my children, intent on raising wholesome, well-rounded women. All brought me awareness, and the promptings of my soul. And then, I took an amazing class on the power of the mind — and viola — it opened… and EXPLODED many doors of awareness.

The light in my heart, the spark in my soul grew brighter. I was unwilling to let the ugly of the past take root and destroy my future.

I remember learning to laugh! Sound strange? I had become so serious that when people around me told jokes, I could not laugh. I didn't see anything funny. Now, it is a different story — I get to enjoy some amazing belly laughs — and what a healer laughter is.

As I maneuvered through life, raising my daughters, I made my fair share of mistakes, but those mistakes were teaching me and preparing me for what life could be and was supposed to be!

All that said, I know beyond all doubt that I do not hold a corner on the market when it comes to the pain I experienced. Many others have experienced the same or worse.

> *"Owning our story can be hard but not as difficult as spending our lives running from it. Exploring and embracing our vulnerabilities is risky but not nearly as dangerous as giving up on love, belonging, and joy — the experiences that make us the most vulnerable. Only when we are brave enough to explore the darkness will we discover the infinite power of our light."*
> — **Brene Brown**

I've observed that often, the women who had the troubled, tough childhoods, are the ones, who today are leading the world in unique and heartfelt ways. They stumbled their way through finding themselves as they stepped into adulthood and, in time, they discovered their strengths and special gifts.

I believe that the inherent goodness of humanity is awakening and that it is time to shine our light out to the world. From the depths of our souls, we can choose to shine. The world needs us. WE need us! We need to embrace the life that makes our hearts sing.

Think about it. Which feels better? Succumbing to the heartache and sadness that too often color our world or choosing to live a joyous and rewarding life?

> *Living our SOUL SHINE*
> *opens our inner world*
> *to possibilities and magic.*

We have an inner glow... a SOUL SHINE... that does not go unnoticed by others. When our personalities become aligned with our souls, our power to attract the desires of our hearts is magnified and optimized. As we begin to live our lives on purpose and joyfully, we create a ripple effect that makes a difference in our lives and the lives of others simply by being ourselves.

It does not require us to be a Mother Teresa *or to be what society has told us we should be* — though if that is what your soul is speaking to you… listen to it.

So what is SOUL SHINE?

SOUL SHINE begins with a glimmer of recognition. A deep inner knowing that there is something more to life. There is something more to YOU.

SOUL SHINE is that inner stirring that wants to be expressed in life. At first, it can feel a bit disconcerting, like a restlessness that won't go away. A gentle knowingness that begins with a little spark that fans into a glowing ember and then a flame when acknowledged.

How Can We Awaken Our SOUL SHINE?

It begins with recognizing yourself. It starts with stopping long enough within our days to listen and watch for clues. It starts with stepping into worthiness. It begins with the willingness to recognize who YOU are and what you stand for.

And often, it is grace through surrender, self-compassion, and self-love. Love — for ourselves can become the master healer of our lives.

No matter what life has brought us, the good, the bad, the ugly, we simply cannot change what has transpired already. What is done is done. Looking back, other than to reflect on how far you have come, and what you learned from those times, will not change anything.

The change happens when we realize that all we have is the here and now. Is it time to feel our way into our SOUL SHINE?

It is time to agree with ourselves to let our SOUL SHINE.

It is through the power of this agreement that our lives become infused with focus, meaning, and direction.

Life has shown me that swimming in the memories and letting the clouds overpower me — is far more painful than letting my SOUL SHINE.

Think about it. We have all heard that it takes more muscles to frown than to smile. With good reason! It certainly feels far better to be happy than sad, to shine than to live a life of dullness and grief.

Sadness and despair become an engrained, deeply entrenched pattern or habit.

And if that is the same for you to a greater or lesser degree, let us explore the world of possibility together.

Don't look away from those moments. Lean into the messiness, the craziest of challenges, the times of feeling lost or deep in self-doubt.

Why? Because those moments illuminate your RADIANT LEGACY… your radiant potentials… your untapped skills, undiscovered possibilities, and under-estimated passions. They lead you to discover what makes **YOUR** SOUL SHINE all that it is.

Dig in. Consider. Embrace. Then, let's link arms and radiate a NEW feminine creative consciousness into the world. Because, SOUL SHINING, incredible (amazing) woman, is what the world needs most now.

Are you open to the idea of letting your SOUL SHINE? Are you willing to grow beyond what perhaps has defined your life till now?

If so, these steps will begin to open the doors and windows of your life.

It begins with asking yourself some pointed questions. But be aware that asking the questions also requires you to listen within for the answers. To hear those answers, we often need to get quiet and pay attention to the sparks of recognition and knowingness that well from within.

Ask yourself:

- *Where do I want to go in life?*
- *What do I desire to create for myself?*
- *Why do I desire this?*
- *How dedicated am I to let my life be incredibly remarkable and spectacular?*
- *How great am I willing to let my life become?*

It is time to shine the light on the shadows of our soul and get real and raw with ourselves. It's time to excavate the roots behind why we are not living the life we are meant to live. The origins of this often dwell in feelings of unworthiness, deservingness, stuckness, and even fear. Fear of change. Fear of letting go.

Ask yourself:

- *Am I underestimating what I am truly willing to receive?*
- *Am I deserving of more?*
- *Am I dreaming big, rich, and juicy enough to flame the spark within me?*
- *Is it time to replace all the un's of negativity with a new energy?*

So now, let's talk about how to implement SOUL SHINE Practices to discover, uncover, and reveal the true you — waiting to ignite that flame into an ember and then into a fire that lights your world.

"When you step into who you really are, everything works."

IGNITING YOUR SHINE WITH SUPERPOWER PRACTICES

What are your superpowers? Do you tap into them daily? What would be a useful superpower in your everyday life?

If you could choose a superpower, what would it be?

The following suggestions are not to overwhelm you. Explore and find what works for YOU. They are meant to spark your SOUL SHINE and expand your mind past the identity that miscreated your childhood and beyond.

It is meant to help you reframe old beliefs, dissolving an outdated mindset that diminishes your creative powers.

Here are just a few Superpower Practices:

1. The Power of the Pause

The power of the pause is well-researched. It promotes relaxation and refreshes you for hours. Both the outer noise and the often more incessant inner noise can keep us from finding the answers we seek.

Power Pause Practice:

- Place your feet on the floor and your hand on your thighs and close your eyes. And if you're driving, just keep your eyes steady
- For a moment, bring your attention way down to your feet. Just notice your feet on the ground,

- notice your seat in the chair, notice your hands on your legs.
- Now find your heart beating, find your pulse somewhere in your body. Bring your mind, your attention, into your body as quickly as possible.
- Now place a light attention on the natural rhythm of your breath. With your mind resting on your breath, you may start to notice a sense of ease. You may start to notice, as you exhale fully, that there's a little bit less tension. A little bit less noise.
- There's not much to do when all you need to do for the next few moments is notice your feet, notice your hands, notice your heartbeat and notice your breath, landing on any one of those areas in your body is just perfect. A perfect way to take a pause.
- And now open your eyes if they have been closed and just notice what a few moments of pause can do. Our bodies are magnificent, brilliant, stabilizing systems when we give our body and our mind the opportunity to balance and align.

2. Surrender

Surrender is what worthiness looks like when a new sense of potential is realized. I invite you to step into the wholeness of worthiness.

Every one of us at some point encounters a situation that rocks the foundation of who we are and what we think we can bear — something that pushes us past our limits. Sometimes it's a situation we've lived with for a long time and sometimes it's a sudden event that overwhelms us and for which our usual coping strategies are useless. Our mind tries to control everything it comes in contact with. And then comes a time, a situation, when we can't keep fighting, either because it's too painful, or because we finally know at a body/heart level that it's futile and some other as of yet unknown path is needed.

Surrender begins here, where all other strategies end. It's waking up to realize that all the strategies have failed and we're plum out of new ones.

Surrender Practice:
To practice, we simply surrender into what is, right now. We drop into our direct experience, what we are sensing, feeling, living in this moment. We agree to feel life, as it is, now, without our mind adding, taking away, manipulating, or doing anything whatsoever to it.

Ask/Invite Yourself:

- *What is it like right now if I let everything be just as it is?*
- *If I don't do anything to it, what is my actual experience in this moment?*
- Feel this, here, now.

Surrender, at its core, is the willingness to meet life as it is, to stop fighting with or trying to change what is so, right now. And remarkably, no matter what the catalyst, or whether it is a moment's surrender or a lifetime's, the result or gift that accompanies it remains the same: relief, gratitude, grace, and sometimes even joy.

3. Trust

Trust is a superpower that is often undervalued. At the foundation of self-confidence and the basis of boldness and self-assertion is a deep inner trust. If trust shuts you down — and it keeps you under lock and key, it is time to unlearn old beliefs. *Why?* Because your current ideas of trust (as in you can only trust yourself) hold you back from experiencing your real, authentic self.

Trust births from a core acknowledged truth: *You are a divine being in physical form.* When you're focused on that major detail, every limitation previously attributed to trusting yourself and others spontaneously melts away.

4. Gratitude

Gratitude is a positive emotion that involves being thankful and appreciative and is associated with several mental and physical health benefits. When you experience gratitude, you feel grateful for something or someone in your life and respond with feelings of kindness, warmth, and other forms of generosity.

So what does gratitude look like? How do you know if you are experiencing a sense of gratitude? Expressing your appreciation and thanks for what you have can happen in a number of different ways. For example, it might entail:

- Spending a few moments thinking about the things in your life that you are grateful for
- Stopping to observe and acknowledge the beauty of wonder of something you encounter in your daily life

- Being thankful for your health
- Thanking someone for the positive influence they have in your life
- Doing something kind for another person to show that you are grateful
- Paying attention to the small things in your life that bring you joy and peace
- Meditation or prayer focused on giving thanks

5. Passion

What is your passion? Passion is a powerful motivator and the essence of commitment. Passion is what stirs us, the fuel for will, the Soul Shine, the fire within. Passion is the seed from which commitment blossoms. Is it time to dream bigger and dance with the possibilities?

> *"There is not passion to be found playing small, in settling for a life that is less that the one you are capable of living."*
> —Nelson Mandela

Following your passion will allow even more creative potential to pave the way to heal, to teach, to inspire and love.

6. Forgiveness

> *"It's one of the greatest gifts you can give yourself. Forgive. Forgive everybody."*
> — Maya Angelou

This important lesson from Maya Angelou is about the importance and power that the act of forgiveness can bring to someone. More importantly — what it can do to help your Soul Shine!

Choosing to forgive someone is an extraordinarily powerful gift, to yourself... first and foremost. In my case, the forgiveness of my father did not come till long after he had passed on. But forgiving him is something I did for myself. It alleviated the constant festering of ugly memories and years of toxic anger, guilt, shame, and fear that had built up inside me. I forgave him for my wellbeing.

It does NOT mean that I condone what he did to myself and my family. It means that there is something inherently strong in being able to say, 'I forgive you', and truly mean it, which yields positive benefits to every facet of your life. Forgiveness is good, so go spread it in your own life as much as you can.

There are so many other superpowers that come into play that will spark that Soul Shine within. It is my heartfelt hope and passion that you will begin to explore what makes your Soul Shine!

I recently attended a class where in a class of ten — every one of us was facing tough issues. The beautiful young woman leading the class taught Somatics... the basics of it being Breath — Sound — Movement — Touch. It sure made a cool difference for each of the attendees.

Many blessings...

Becky

Radiant Reset Journaling

The following are journaling prompts designed to reveal your soul shine.

It is my intention to inspire you to explore your own relationship with the shine of your soul in ways that will elevate your life.

What does soul shine mean to you?

___
___
___
___
___
___
___
___
___
___
___
___
___
___
___
___
___
___

Becky Norwood

Where do you see your life five years from now?

What are your superpowers? How can recognizing and using your super-powers empower you with soul shine?

Becky Norwood

What practices will you commit to that will help your soul shine?

How great are you willing to let your life become?

About Becky Norwood

Becky Norwood is a multi-published #1 International Bestselling author, speaker, & book publishing expert.

Her passion is helping women discover, uncover, and recover their Soul Shine, find their authentic voice, and lead in the world with radiant passion.

She is widely recognized for the empowering and intuitive way she guides others to weave storytelling into a powerful way to build a legacy and gateway for the healing and growth of themselves, their families, and the world. In sharing authentic, vulnerable, stories they can impact others to ignite that flame into an ember and then into a fire that lights their own world. She is an advocate for the positive that comes from letting your SOUL SHINE.

To learn more about Becky Norwood and her work visit:

Website: https://spotlightpublishinghouse.com
Email: becky@spotlightpublishinghouse.com
Facebook: https://www.facebook.com/SpotlightBookPublishing
LinkedIn: https://www.linkedin.com/in/beckybnorwood/
YouTube: https://www.youtube.com/channel/UCnsI302EpaLWPnRJxwaq-tA
Instagram: https://www.instagram.com/spotilghtpublishinghouse/

Dedicated to those who have poured their hearts into love, given endlessly, and embraced every moment with joy — yet somehow lost sight of themselves along the way.

To those now walking the path of self-discovery, learning to cultivate a deep and loving relationship with themselves; to those determined to honor their true essence, embrace self-love wholeheartedly, and stand unwavering and unwilling to negotiate the heart of who they are.

And, never to be forgotten, love and respect to my family and friends who have loved me throughout every chapter of my journey.

Debra Shoults Bettendorf

Chapter 6

The Most Important Relationship You'll Ever Have

Debra Shoults Bettendorf

*When self-reflection and self-honor come together,
we gain the power to build a deeper connection
with our true selves.
It's in this natural growth...
owning who we are...
that we find the courage
and sometimes the confidence
to no longer be willing to negotiate
the calling of our soul... the heart of who we are.*

Today I feel more confident with myself than I ever have but that didn't come without commitment to self-reflection and self-honor. And that self-reflection began with being unwilling to negotiate who I am.

*True self-honor began with being
unwilling to negotiate who I am.*

Looking back on my younger self, I can see how much I longed for self-acceptance and for others to like me. Maybe what I was really searching for was belonging. While wanting to be liked is a natural human instinct, it's important not to lose sight of your authentic self in the process. I've always enjoyed having friends, supporting them, and celebrating their successes. Eventually, I came to understand that while I often did this for others, I rarely did it for myself. I had somehow persuaded myself that significant achievements were reserved for others.

This brings me to another thought:

Did I believe those lofty dreams and achievements weren't meant for me?

Was I afraid that being too successful would make me less liked?

After a lot of introspection, I've come to understand that both were true for me.

Over the years, I've gradually reconnected with my true, authentic self — the woman who knows she has so much to offer and embraces her unique qualities. I've cherished every decade of my life, and being a wife and mother brought me great joy, as it still does. However, when the kids left for college, I found myself wondering who I was outside of the role I had embraced for nearly twenty years. That was when I began a journey of self-discovery, searching for Debbie — not just the mom, wife, friend, sister or daughter. While I know I am all of these, I began to ask myself... *When everything else is stripped away, who am I, and what do I truly enjoy?*

Asking myself the question, "Who am I?"
This is when the door opened to
finding forgotten aspects of myself.

As the kids were growing up, I was constantly involved in their activities and school life. I loved being a room mom, driving on field trips, and helping the children at school with their "book-it" reading programs. My husband and I also volunteered to work bingo one Saturday a month to help raise funds for their parochial school. Every year, we had Dinner Auctions, and I enjoyed contributing to that, especially in reaching out to local businesses to donate items and then setting things up.

Outside of school, I often organized projects for my kids to create Easter, Christmas, or Thanksgiving gifts to deliver to nursing homes or bring essential items to families in need. This was something I deeply valued, and I wanted my children to understand the importance of helping others.

What I discovered is that I have
a need and desire to fill up my cup
of what brings me greater connection with myself.

I also had a strong interest in our community and became a member of the Junior Civic League. Each year, we hosted a Gala, which required a great deal of effort, but it supported many wonderful causes in the community. Helping others has always brought me joy.

As I write this, I am remembering all of the times I picked up random people off of the street to take them where they needed to go. That was until I gave a ride to someone who scared me a little bit, so I stopped doing that. (funny not funny)

I've always loved being there for my friends and family, offering a listening ear or advice when needed. Being part of something that makes a positive impact on others' lives feels like home to my soul. After the kids went off to college and I began to explore who "Debbie" truly is, I realized that I've always enjoyed being a source of comfort and support for others.

Another passion of mine is fashion. I decided to combine my love for helping women with my love for fashion by starting an image consulting business. This allowed me to spend time with women, helping them not only look fabulous in their clothes but also feel fabulous in their hearts.

The interesting thing about starting my image consulting business is that I had been considering it for a few months, even coming up with the name *"Find Your Fabulous,"* but I hadn't leaped. On a flight home from Los Angeles, I was seated next to a woman, and after about an hour, we started chatting. She worked for Camp Empowerment in Malibu, a camp where women go to rediscover themselves. I found it fascinating, as I was in a similar place in my life.

When she asked me what I did, I shared my idea for the business. She listened and then asked why I hadn't just gone for it. She reminded me that it's better to try than to sit in a rocking chair one day, looking back and wishing I had. While this wasn't a new concept to me, sometimes you hear the right words at the right time from the right person, and it really makes an impact. Within a week of landing, I registered the business and officially launched *"Find Your Fabulous."*

Is it possible that the more you discover what brings you joy is also a discovery of a sense of belonging and purpose?

That has been over a decade ago, and where am I now? There have been so many experiences, life happenings and lessons. As I remember, I cry and then I remember another memory and feel the urge to laugh. There have been happy times and there has been loss. Through it all I choose to believe that there are lessons learned and definitely from them I am wiser. The more I learn the more I realize how much more I need to learn. Learn? Yes, learn even more about who I am. I have heard people say, "It's like peeling back layers of an onion." I totally understand that now. We all have many layers and sometimes pulling those layers back will bring tears to our eyes.

I have some questions for you.

Do you have a good relationship with yourself?
Do you really know yourself? What brings you the most joy?

Try not answer with: "It brings joy to me to see my kids (parents, partner…) happy." *Outside of everyone or everything, what brings YOU joy? What do you enjoy doing?*

I believe that it is valuable, I would say even crucial to know yourself and know what brings you joy before you can fully be present for yourself and others.

For years I basically found joy in bringing others joy. I still do. The difference in Debbie then and Debbie now is I take notice of the things that bring me happiness that doesn't result by doing something for others. Helping others is incredibly important and I am not dismissing that. In fact, the reason I'm writing this is in the hope that sharing my experiences might help someone else — and that would bring me, you guessed it... joy. However, I find joy in being outside in nature, taking a brisk walk, meditating, praising God and keeping a gratitude journal. I love to stretch and raise my arms over my head and take deep breaths. I enjoy making a deal with myself to drink plenty of water and then actually drinking it.

I love my morning coffee and dousing it with cinnamon, collagen and almond milk among other things some days. I love to write, a passion that was hidden or buried for many years. Rediscovering who I am has brought me back to it, and it feels really fulfilling.

Who were you before the world told you that you couldn't?

Remember with me. *When you were a child, did you have big dreams? Can you even remember them?* In either case, it is never too late to dream big and go for it. Dream now and put a little action behind it. This isn't a pep talk even though it is lending itself to that. This is real, the truth that I want to share.

I can't tell you have many times I have written for this book only to sit down later and read it over and realize that it sounded like a biography and so I have switched gears. This is definitely about me and my experiences; however, I want to bring you along with me. The more I know the more I know there is so much more to learn, more to know.

My children have always asked me why I turn everything in life into a lesson. As they were growing up and something didn't go in their favor or they made a mistake, I would always give them a scenario of how this is helping them. I was not always their favorite person and I know they were rolling their eyes. I know one thing for sure and that is we will experience good times and we will experience bad times and we can choose to learn from it and somehow try to find the positives. My children have observed difficult situations in my life. They've seen me become emotional at first, but also witnessed how I rise above them, using those experiences as opportunities to grow and become a better person.

They have seen, a time or two, someone not be so nice to me and I have not ridiculed or talked negatively about them. I have been asked how I handle that and I can tell you that being mean or retaliating would never make me feel any better.

Finding the path to belonging isn't always easy...
it is an understanding of the power of the challenging
circumstances that may be paved in perceived
failure and disappointments.

What is important is gaining an understanding of the challenging circumstances and finding the lesson, the learning, the wisdom inside of it.

What is Soul Searching?

For me, soul searching is when you are going along in life seemingly happy, but there is a feeling that something is missing. I couldn't quite put my finger on it and I continued to pray about it and also sit in stillness with myself. I would take notes of how I was feeling and write in length in my journal. I would write almost every day. It was cathartic. It almost felt like a beautiful release… a release of getting something out that needed to be said or the feeling you get after a good workout. Writing thoughts and experiences along with feelings in a journal is therapeutic for me but it is also fascinating to revisit it later. It offers valuable insight into who we are. It was those writings that propelled me into writing my first book.

My book was inspired by my first business, *Find Your Fabulous: Love Yourself on the Inside and Look Great on the Outside.* I wanted this book to feel like a personal conversation, similar to my journal entries — genuine and straightforward. I tackled the important topic of self-love, presenting it in a simplified, approachable way that isn't overwhelming. And, of course, I included some fashion tips along the way.

I put myself out there and published the book because I promised myself I would, and I wanted to prove to myself that I could follow through. By doing so, I also opened the door to others' opinions — whether they believed I was worthy of being an author or wondered, *"Who does she think she is to publish a book?"* The good news is, I'm okay with that. I understand that putting yourself out there comes with the risk of criticism. The former Debbie sought approval and wanted to be loved by everyone, but she now knows that's not realistic. Now, I'm focused on shining in all areas of my life and rediscovering the God-given strengths I'd forgotten or pushed aside. I'm curious: *What strengths have you forgotten?*

Sharing this with you is incredibly difficult for me. Even though I have come a long way, articulating my innermost feelings and insecurities is not easy.

But it is in the innate rising… owning who we are… that's where we find the courage and sometimes the confidence to no longer be willing to negotiate the calling of our soul… the heart of who we are.

Throughout my journey, I've experienced powerful signs and synchronicities affirming that I'm on the right path. I had actively sought these signs, and they've appeared in abundance. One especially profound experience was shared in the pages of the first edition of *Amazing Woman Divine Legacy, A New Era of Feminine Prosperity*. I treasured this experience privately for a long time. Only a few people knew. I shared this with Marsh and she told me, *'If you've learned what you needed from it, then it's time to share.'* So, I did, feeling both vulnerable and confident as I put myself out there once again.

I decided to start my podcast, FIND IT, where I bring on guests to share how they've discovered something valuable in their lives — whether it's success in their career, fitness, health, faith, relationships, or other areas. My goal is for the audience to find inspiration and guidance through these stories.

Naturally, starting the podcast sparked conversations, with some people questioning why I was doing a podcast and wondering *"Who does she think she is?"* But I'm okay with that. I love meeting people and, even more, learning from them. I'm constantly inspired by the successes of others.

Bringing ourselves to a deeper sense of belonging (with ourselves, the belonging of self), taking a stand for our deeper callings and acting on our desires can sometimes look like, "Who does she think she is" to others. While all the while our actions are taking us along a path to our desired destiny.

If I hadn't started the podcast, I would never have met Marsh Engle, and I wouldn't be contributing to this book today. I also want to share a meaningful synchronicity: after publishing my first book, I said to myself, "I'm going to write another book, and it will be a bestseller." Well, the book I was a contributing author with Marsh in 2024 became a bestseller. That's some powerful manifesting! I am putting this out there right now too, this book is a Bestseller!

I've learned to trust myself. One of my God-given strengths is an innate ability to understand or sense things deeply. I have a natural empathy for others, even when I haven't personally experienced their pain. I receive intuitive feelings or a knowing that I used to doubt because they didn't seem logical. Now, I am listening to my intuition more and placing greater trust in myself. Speaking of empathy-that is something I have given freely to others and learning to do more for myself as well.

Paying attention to the little things can help us uncover the power of the more meaningful things.

In May 2023, I experienced a health scare. Thankfully, everything turned out fine, and it made me pause to appreciate life and reflect on my journey. There were a few things I'd always wanted to pursue but had held back, uncertain of my chances of success. This moment reminded me of past lessons about pushing through fear and just going for it. So, I decided to launch *Studio 11 Style*.

Life is precious and not guaranteed.
Live your life authentically you.
We must live our lives for ourselves,
live authentically and not for someone else.

Aligned with my belief that life's experiences are meant to help us grow, learn, and find the positives, I'm fully immersed in the journey of building my new business, *Studio 11 Style*. With all the work and learning involved, I remind myself once again that I've moved beyond fear and self-doubt to make this vision a reality. I've created a fashion haven for women that goes beyond style; it's a community where women uplift one another, encouraging self-love and celebrating our unique strengths and contributions. The tagline *"On a scale from 1 to 10, you're an 11"* is a reminder that we are beyond any standard scale. It encourages us not to conform to expectations of how we "should" be, but rather to focus on being the very best version of ourselves.

As I reflect on those times when I felt like something was missing, I now realize it was me that was missing… I missed you. I was missing the woman I knew I could be. The woman who took chances, dreamed big, and valued those dreams. The woman who said yes to herself and had the confidence to go for it. I am taking chances, knowing that even if it fails, it is not a failure. Putting action behind my dreams is a win. Cheers to an ongoing and nurturing relationship with myself. It isn't a perfect relationship and there are no expectations for it to be.

Having a trusting relationship with ourselves is so important.

I am sharing a few things that helped me and are continuing to help me form a better relationship with myself and live a more authentic life.

- I am honoring my experiences and understanding that I am part of a new era of women leaders.
- I am realizing that I have been on the path of creating my divine legacy all along.
- I give honor and gratitude to all that has already been manifested and completed.
- I know that this acknowledgment and appreciation propels me to create at a higher level.

*I said to myself that I wanted to write a book, and I did it.
This is important because
I know when I set a goal for myself,
I can trust that I will do it.
Having that trusting relationship
will ourselves is so important.
In a world where you cannot always trust others,
we can trust ourselves.*

When I slow down and recognize and acknowledge my own progress, it gives way to higher self-worth. Progress looks different for each of us. When you're pushing yourself toward a task or goal, remember to recognize and appreciate each achievement, no matter how small. It might mean going to the gym for a workout for the first time — taking that first step is significant, so celebrate it. Or maybe it's finding time for yourself to relax, read a book, light a candle, and enjoy some stillness. Show gratitude for that effort toward self-care. In my case, I have been on a path to rediscover who I am and put effort into connecting with self.

*I've found that the more I express
gratitude for the small wins,
the more positivity I attract into my life.*

Each year, I choose a word to guide me through the upcoming months. This year, my word is "intention." I want to be mindful of my choices and ensure each one has purpose and meaning. I am open to the endless possibilities within myself and ready to embrace them thoughtfully and intentionally.

I am thankful for the time I've invested in my personal growth.

Here are some truths I've discovered along the way.

Self-Awareness
Focus on what brings you joy independent of others and external influences.

Ask: *What unique talents do you possess?*

This practice of acquiring self-awareness helps you identify what truly makes you happy and, if you're uncertain, can guide you toward discovering it.

Self-awareness in all areas of our lives is so important.

Ask yourself in situations that anger you, make you sad or happy... Why?

If we are aware and honest with ourselves,
that is where the growth happens.

Learner's Mindset
Approach new experiences with confidence, be ready to try things out, learn as you go, and refine what works and what doesn't.

Once you pay attention and truly listen to learn, you can find personal growth through their experiences.

Intention / Vision
Be open and willing to see the endless possibilities and potentials within and around you. Allow yourself to dream boldly, to envision a future aligned with your values and passions, and to pursue it with purpose. Trust that by setting meaningful intentions, you can create a path that brings these possibilities to life.

I have learned that big dreams belong to me, too.
They belong to each of us.

Action
Be ready to take steps toward what you want, bravely and without hesitation. Be willing to act, even when you are unsure because you know each step brings you closer to your goals. Trust yourself to make choices, learn along the way, and keep moving forward with determination.

It's often said that the longest relationship
you'll ever have is with yourself.
Imagine what your life will be when you actively
nurture this relationship and continuously discover
more about yourself as you navigate life…
Truly, becoming a better version of yourself as you
connect more deeply with who you are…
owning your thoughts, standing firm in your beliefs,
and feeling confident in holding your truth
without feeling the need to explain or justify.
When you compromise just to please others,
what does that really accomplish?

I'm staying true to myself, and if others can't accept that, that's okay. We teach people how to treat us. If we tolerate bad behavior or let others speak negatively to us without expressing our discomfort, some people may continue treating us that way, justifying it by assuming that our silence means their behavior is acceptable. It's possible to express your dislike calmly and without confrontation although speaking up can feel uncomfortable or awkward. I'm still learning to appreciate the beauty of self-honor, and it feels empowering to know that I'm respecting myself enough to prioritize my well-being over simply pleasing others.

*I'm on a mission to live my most authentic life
and to inspire as many people as possible to do the same.
I bring a vibrant, energetic spirit and believe
we can live our best lives at any age.
I enjoy spreading positivity and love.*

*How do I feel about myself since taking
this deep dive into who "Debbie" truly is?*

I feel a sense of fulfillment in my soul's purpose. I am continuously growing into who I am and I am aware that I am constantly changing and evolving into a more positive change for the world. I never remain stagnant in a position; I learn, I open myself up to the guidance and protection of God. I support other women by encouraging and celebrating their authenticity at every age. I revel in recognition with a humble and grateful heart.

I have a book full of my writings, and it's inspiring to look back and read them. I encourage you to express your positive thoughts and desires as well. Often, we reveal insights to ourselves through our own words. You may notice recurring thoughts and feelings that increase self-awareness, helping you connect with who you truly are and identify areas to address or work through. When we commit to discovering our authentic selves, doing the inner work, and accepting that it may feel uncomfortable, we rise to the challenge and find fulfillment in life.

My wish is that each woman finds sheer joy in her journey as she reveals a true sense of belonging within herself.

Here's to living in authenticity, honoring ourselves fully, and embracing the courage to pursue our true paths without fear or hesitation. May we find strength in being our truest selves, purpose in every challenge, and joy in every step we take toward fulfilling our potential. Cheers to the journey of self-discovery, resilience, and boldness in doing all that we're meant to do.

I feel like we always want a great ending to our story… but maybe what we are truly seeking is living with our heart in every moment, in every action, in every connection. That is what I wish for you… sheer joy in your journey.

Radiant Reset Journaling

On the following pages, you'll find journaling prompts.

Each question is designed to build a deeper connection with your true self.

It is my intention to inspire you to find the courage and the confidence to no longer negotiate the calling of your soul… the heart of who you are.

What is one thing you are no longer willing to negotiate?

Debra Shoults Bettendorf

What brings you joy?

Did you know that happiness is not present in difficult times but Joy can be.

Debra Shoults Bettendorf

What were your childhood dreams for your future?

_____
_____
_____
_____
_____
_____
_____
_____
_____
_____
_____
_____
_____
_____
_____
_____
_____
_____

Debra Shoults Bettendorf

Are you able to trust yourself? What is something that you told yourself you were going to do and followed through? How did that make you feel? Did you give yourself a lot of love for that?

Debra Shoults Bettendorf

Do you have a good relationship with yourself? Why or why not?

___
___
___
___
___
___
___
___
___
___
___
___
___
___
___
___
___
___
___

Debra Shoults Bettendorf

About Debra Shoults Bettendorf

"For as long as I can remember I've envisioned a day when women will joyfully bring their inner beauty to their outer beauty… now through Studio 11 Style I'm helping women do exactly that."

As a fashion entrepreneur and founder of Studio 11 Style, Debra Shoults Bettendorf is devoted to ensuring every woman feels valued, empowered and fabulous within. Studio 11 Style's tagline, "On a Scale From 1 to 10, You're an 11," serves as a powerful reminder that we rise above ordinary standards. It highlights our unique essence and reminds us that we are far beyond what we often perceive ourselves to be.

Her strong commitment to female empowerment drives her to cultivate an ever-growing supportive community where women celebrate each other's achievements and embrace their unique strengths. As host of the popular podcast series, *FIND IT!* she calls upon her deep empathetic nature to connect with people on a deeply intimate level while providing a platform for voices and views to be shared, fostering open dialogue, personal growth, and mutual respect.

Her book, *Find Your Fabulous: Love Yourself on the Inside, Look Great on the Outside* is a blend of heart and soul with a dose of fashion… and is filled with an abundance of positivity, charm, and wit. Debra believes you are never too young or too old to *Find Your Fabulous*.

Debra was a contributing author in the bestselling book, *Amazing Woman Divine Legacy* and is a featured co-author in the second in the *Amazing Woman Divine Legacy* Series: *The Radiant Reset* "Reshaping a New Narrative of Sacred Confidence and the Radiant Power to Serve the World."

To learn more about Debra Bettendorf and her work visit: www.findyourfabulous11.com

I dedicate this chapter to my mother Joann Jackson.
She taught me the beauty of being kind to others.

Candice Smith Güzelişik

Chapter 7

Divine Potential

Lessons From Women Past & Present

Candice Smith Güzelişik

> *"Who is She?*
> *She is your power,*
> *your Feminine source.*
> *Big Mama. The Goddess.*
> *The Great Mystery.*
> *The web-weaver.*
> *The life force.*
> *The first time, the twentieth time*
> *you may not recognize her.*
> *Or pretend not to hear.*
> *As she fills your body with ripples of terror and delight.*
> *But when she calls you will know you've been called.*
> *Then it is up to you to decide if you will answer."*
> —Lucy H. Pearce

When I think of divine potential, I immediately think of how strongly rooted it is in one's divine purpose. We all come into this physical experience with a specific purpose, a purpose for our individual journey, and a purpose for how we can create an impact on those around us. The ripple effect that leaves a powerful imprint on humanity.

For this reason, each of us has an infinite amount of potential that we have been given.

> *By owning our own personal power,*
> *we can collectively create a ripple effect of*
> *high vibration, love, and positive transformation.*

As it relates to being a woman, our divine potential is particularly important for us to understand how to tap into this resource not only to elevate our soul journey but to step forth as the great manifestors that as women we were created to be. You see the feminine is a special representation of the divine creator, and your divine potential is a sacred gift.

> *Our feminine nature is far from weak.*
> *It is a mirror image of the Divine creator.*
> *It is a sacred gift you've been given to express and share.*

I distinctly remember being in my mid 20s completely dissatisfied with my life. Although I had graduated from college, I didn't feel particularly accomplished. I had been working in various companies doing call center work and though the wage was decent (or so I thought at the time), the work was unfulfilling, and I was oftentimes left wondering if *this* was what would become of my life. I would quiet the voice in my heart that wanted more out of life by telling myself that I should be grateful for what I had and that where I was in my life should be enough, but it wasn't.

One early morning as I was clocking into work at 6 a.m. the revelation hit me like a ton of bricks. This could not be my life. Did people seriously just wake up, go to a lackluster job, eat, take care of their kids, go to sleep, get a paycheck every other week, spend a bit of time with their family, scrape by financially, and repeat the cycle over and over until they take their last breath?

I swear in that moment of swiping in at the time clock, my future seemed to flash before my eyes and what I saw scared me. It scared me so much that I asked the universe a question that forever transformed my life. That question: What is my purpose in life? For the first time, I heard an answer loud and clear. My purpose was to help women feel beautiful on the inside and out.

It seems the moment I became clear about my purpose, opportunities for me to use my talents, and all the potential that I had been given were coming my way at god-speed. I was finally ready to give birth to all that I had dreamed of, and all that I was meant to be.

A woman's potential is like a woman's eggs, being safely stored until the proper time to be released. Either the egg will be fertilized and birthed as a baby, or it will be shed during a woman's menstrual phase of her cycle.

> *Unlike a woman's eggs, which are limited in number, your potential is limitless and your potential to birth many things into existence is one of the most exciting and important things you can do as a woman.*

It's one of our superpowers as a woman. The gift of creating from our womb space, be it dreams or babies is a magical process that can only happen when we tap into the power of our potential.

There was an anti-drug campaign years ago during the 80's about the mind being a terrible thing to waste. I feel the same way about a woman wasting her potential.

Far too many women waste their divine potential due to lack of courage, fear of failing, listening to the wrong voices, self-sabotage, majoring in the minors, not being clear about their life's purpose, and not understanding why their soul was brought forth as a woman. I believe this is at the foundation of why women are settling for the bare minimum in life or the *"good enough"* in life, depression, anxiety, imposter syndrome, and poor quality of life.

The older I get the more wisdom I collect. The more countries I travel to, I realize that being a woman is truly a special gift. We are here as a special representation of divine creator energy. We are the representation of portals for physical existence and high levels of manifestations. And in embracing this powerful part of womanhood you will be able to awaken your divine potential in a way you never could before.

The wonderful thing about life
is that there is nothing new under the sun,
and there have always been women
have shown us the way.

If we take a closer look at these women closely, we can learn the tools we need to create a life, a home, a career, a business, or anything else we want to create with joy and ease. Let's take a look at some of the women who have paved the path before us and shown us the way.

Frida Kahlo
The Palette of Pain and the Art of Healing

Frida Kahlo's life is a true example of trading ashes for beauty. Born July 6th, 1907 in Coyoacan, Mexico, she suffered a life of physical pain after a tragic traffic accident when she was young. The injuries she suffered left her not only physically impaired but infertile.

Frida used her art as an expression
of her vulnerability and emotions,
She mastered alchemizing her pain into power.

I think every woman has that defining moment in her life where she is left with the choice of letting a painful situation or life event destroy her or transform her into a better and more resilient woman. For me that was my divorce, my then-husband had come home a week before graduating from his aviation program and told me that he was leaving me. I wasn't entirely surprised as our entire marriage had been a rollercoaster, particularly trying when he decided to go back to school to pursue a career as an aviation mechanic.

Up until that point, he had been telling me that once he finished school we would work on our marriage, but it became glaringly clear in that moment as I sat on the sofa listening to him fumble over his words, that this had been his plan the entire time. He had only said those things to keep the peace so that he could finish school, and once he had secured a higher-paying job, he knew he could leave. I was just a stepping-stone in his path and the rejection cut my heart like a knife.

As I discovered more about his plans to leave me, including his saving up over $5,000 so he could relocate, I fell into a deep depression that shifted my emotional state. It took over two years for me to move through the depression and rejection. I had to decide to not let this emotionally crushing moment define who I was, or what I would become in life. I understood that every relationship we have is to help grow us as individuals and that instead of staying hurt and emotionally stuck, I could take that pain and use it as a catalyst to be a better and more refined woman.

Through that experience, I learned to be vulnerable, tap into my community of sisters for support, and to open my heart, and expand my ability to love. The ending of that relationship was the beginning of a brand-new path for me to walk in my divine purpose. Looking back on that situation I am filled with deep gratitude because if he hadn't left, I would have wasted my time and energy living a mediocre life and giving away my feminine energy to someone who didn't deserve it.

Lessons for Modern Women
Walking in Divine Feminine Energy and Purpose

When I reflect on the contributions of this remarkable woman there are five major takeaways that we can apply as women to start using our divine potential.

1. *Alchemize Your Pain into Power:* When we experience something extremely painful in life, it is easy to get stuck, especially if we experience a pain that is life altering like the death of a loved one, a devastating illness, the loss of a job, financial ruin, a divorce or breakup. From Frida we learn that by allowing yourself to deeply feel that pain, you can find ways to transmute that pain into something profound, powerful, pivotal, and potent. We cannot completely avoid pain in life. Life has its winter season, but you can always make the choice to utilize the emotions and lessons of that season to blossom into the woman you were called forth to be.

2. *Embrace Your Authenticity:* I'm not sure if Frida realized just how ahead of her time she was, but it's clear she danced to the beat of her own drum. She embraced who she was unapologetically and serves as a brilliant example of achieving greatness simply by being your imperfect, messy self, and living your truth and standing up for the things you deeply believe in. Far too many people in this world are scared of what others think to stand up for what they believe in and to live their truth. Random strangers and people who wouldn't care if you were homeless, or didn't have food to eat are holding you back

from being the most authentic version of yourself. Work through this fear and the need for validation to find the confidence you need to live out loud.

3. *Embody Self-Love and Care:* Frida nurtured her spirit through art, fashion, and self-expression. Following her example of self-care, we can be inspired as women to prioritize our own needs, foster self-compassion, and celebrate our emotions, bodies and souls as an integral part of our individual and collective journey as women.

4. *Embrace Feminine Energy and Community:* I have always said that embodied feminine women build bridges and community and Frida was most certainly a champion of women. She rallied for women's rights and she engaged with other women and celebrated femininity in her work. Her life encourages us to connect with each other as women, share our experiences with one another, prioritize nurturing our friendships, and support each other's journeys. In doing these things we can cultivate the power of community and embrace the divine feminine energy.

5. *Cultivate Resilience:* Despite Frida facing numerous hardships, including health issues, and a tumultuous relationship with her husband Diego, she showed resilience. Her life serves as an example of how you can't keep a good woman down for long. Perseverance in the face of adversity and rising above the challenges of life with determination is the legacy that Frida Khol left for all of us to live by.

Empress Theodora
It Doesn't Matter Where You Start, As Long As You Get There.

Empress Theodora is a little-known she-ro of her day. Wife of Emperor Justinian I and co-ruler of the Byzantine Empire (527–548 AD), she is a beautiful example of starting from humble beginnings, rising to power, and walking in her divine purpose. Not much is known about her early life, but it is said that before her meeting Emperor Justinian, she worked as an actress and prostitute and that for her to get married to the Emperor special laws had to be passed and they had to receive special permission from the church for the marriage to be valid.

The Emperor not only fell in love with her beauty, but also her intellect, and she became one of his top and most trusted advisors. Many historians think it was she who was truly ruling the country as her name was on the majority of laws passed during that time, and not only did she receive visits from foreign rulers, but she would also correspond with them, all of these tasks normally reserved for the Emperor.

She used her power to advocate for the women in her kingdom by prohibiting the sex trafficking of young girls and giving women more rights and protection under the law when it came to divorce. In fact between her death and the death of Emperor Justinian, there was not a single piece of significant legislation passed, proving that her energy was significant.

There are so many lessons we can learn from Empress Theodora's life force essence. She is a beautiful and powerful example of truly believing that you are a vessel for change and good. Do you understand what it must have taken for her to overcome societal stigma to step into her purpose and become the pinnacle of power at that time in history?

Empress Theodora's story deeply resonates with me, because it reminds me of my own humble beginnings of growing up in the inner-city neighborhoods of Cleveland, Ohio. I lived down the street from an active crack house, and during the early 90's the neighborhood was a hotbed for drugs and sometimes gang violence. I always knew that I was meant for more than what my environment offered, and my mother always encouraged my brother and me to do well in school.

Each day when I walked to my bus stop, I would walk past that crack house and remind myself that I was going to get out of this neighborhood and do great things with my life. I would work hard in school and at one point I took an after-school job to help pay for extra-curricular activities. After graduating from high school and going on to attend college, eventually becoming a successful entrepreneur.

I remember a few years back when I moved to Rome, Italy, I came across an old photo of the house I grew up in back in Cleveland. As a young girl, I could have never imagined the books I would write, places I would travel to, or the lives of women I would change simply by taking a step on faith and daring to believe that I was put here to do something good with my one beautiful life. Empress Theodora reminds us that it doesn't matter where you start, as long as you get there.

Lessons for Modern Women:
Walking in Divine Feminine Energy and Purpose

1. *Embrace Your Power and Purpose*
Empress Theodora's life demonstrates the importance of recognizing and stepping into your power, no matter your starting point. She rose from being a prostitute and performer — a position often stigmatized in her era — to becoming one of the most influential women in history. Theodora did not allow societal labels or expectations to limit her ambitions. Instead, she leveraged her beauty, intelligence, charisma, and resilience to reshape her narrative and carve out her role as a leader.

> *"My entire life changed the moment*
> *I decided to walk in my purpose.*
> *When I accepted my divine mission,*
> *the universe responded*
> *by opening doors and moving me into rooms*
> *I never dreamed of being in."*

- Self-Awareness: Take the time to reflect on your unique talents and strengths. What drives you? What gifts do you bring to the table that no one else can?
- Setting Intentions: Define a clear purpose for your life. This doesn't have to be a grand, sweeping vision — it could be as simple as contributing to your family, community, or profession in a way that feels meaningful.

- Owning Your Narrative: Don't let past hurts, experiences or societal expectations define you. You are on your unique life journey, and you have the power to rewrite your story. Release any guilt from your past. It's all a part of your journey, and you control the narrative. Nobody can shame you about the things you have made peace with.

2. *Balance Strength with Compassion*
Theodora exemplified the ability to lead with both authority and empathy. She enacted sweeping social and legal reforms, particularly those that uplifted women and marginalized groups while maintaining her poise as a ruler. Her actions showed that true leadership doesn't come from brute force but from a deep understanding of the needs of those you serve.

> *"If you want people to follow you,*
> *treat them with kindness,*
> *show that you care about*
> *the things they care about."*

- Empathy in Leadership: Whether you're leading a team, a family, or your own life, remember that strength is amplified by understanding and kindness. Take time to truly listen and respond to others' needs.
- Setting Boundaries: Compassion doesn't mean being a doormat. Theodora's ability to navigate court politics and crises with strategic decision-making shows the importance of standing firm in your convictions.

- Fostering Relationships: Use your influence to build connections and create environments where others can thrive, but don't forget to prioritize self-respect and your own needs.

3. Advocate for Others

One of Empress Theodora's greatest legacies is her unwavering commitment to advocacy. She championed the rights of women, including protecting them from exploitation, improving property rights, and fighting against human trafficking. Her actions remind us that power and privilege come with a responsibility to uplift others, and a failure to do, is a misdeed to humanity.

Modern Application:
- Mentorship: Offer your knowledge and guidance to those who could benefit from your experience. This could be formal, like mentoring in a professional setting, or informal, such as supporting a friend.
- Speaking Up: Use your voice to call out injustices or highlight overlooked issues, especially in spaces where others might not have the opportunity to speak.
- Building Communities: Create or join groups that empower and advocate for shared goals. Collaboration amplifies impact.

"Don't be afraid to ask for what you need along the way. What's the worst they can say? No? It just means they aren't the right person. Keep asking until you get a yes."

Theodora's marriage to Justinian was truly a partnership of equals. She didn't settle for being a figurehead; she actively shaped policies and decisions alongside him. Her self-assurance and recognition of her value allowed her to contribute meaningfully to the empire's success.

> *"It took most of my 20s for me to realize that I had value and that I deserve to have a seat at the table."*

- Demand Equality: In your relationships — whether professional, romantic, or social — expect to be treated with respect and as an equal. Do not shrink yourself to make others comfortable.
- Recognize Your Value: Understand your worth and what you bring to every situation. Advocate for yourself, when necessary, whether it's negotiating a salary, setting boundaries, or pursuing opportunities. Know that you deserve to have a seat at the table.
- Partnerships with Purpose: Align yourself with people who respect and complement your strengths. Whether in business or love, seek partners who empower you rather than diminish you.

> *"Never forget the power of collaboration. I have accomplished my biggest dreams and goals by joining forces with other women."*

One of Theodora's most defining moments came during the Nika Revolt when she refused to flee alongside others, famously declaring that she would rather die as an empress than live in exile. Her unwavering courage not only stabilized the empire but also solidified her legacy as a leader who stood firm in her purpose.

> *"Over the years I have learned to trust myself, trust my gut. The more in tune you become with your feminine intuition you can trust what your body is trying to tell you and take risks and decisions from an intuitive place."*

- Face Challenges Head-On: When adversity strikes, remind yourself of your resilience. Courage isn't about the absence of fear but about moving forward despite it.
- Trust Your Intuition: Theodora's ability to assess situations and make bold decisions was rooted in her confidence in her own judgment. Hone your intuition and trust it to guide you.
- Take Calculated Risks: Don't be afraid to take calculated risks. Sometimes you must walk out in faith knowing that all of the energy you've put out in the universe will be returned.

Empress Theadora was a woman of incredible vision, resilience, and influence who embodied divine feminine energy to shape history. Her story inspires modern women to lead with purpose, strength, and grace. Embrace your inner Theodora — walk confidently in your divine feminine energy, live with intention, and let your purpose shape the world around you.

Oprah Winfrey
Writing Her Own Narrative, A Masterclass in Purpose-Driven Power

Oprah Winfrey's life is one of the ultimate rags-to-riches stories. Born in the rural, racially segregated south of the United States in the 50s and enduring sexual abuse and teen pregnancy, Oprah Winfrey defied all odds becoming a local news anchor and slowly rising to the *Queen of All Media* with her talk show The Oprah Winfrey show.

What made Oprah stand out from the crowd was her dedication to sharing people's stories with compassion and empathy and staying true to her purpose. Over the years she has risen to not only become one of the world's wealthiest women but to become a true spiritual leader.

She often talks about the importance of walking in our purpose and owning our personal power. She is a true example of how the universal powers open when you stand firm in who you were called forth to be.

Oprah has always been an incredible source of encouragement for me. I remember when I was working through my childhood trauma in my early 20's I remember watching an episode of the Oprah Winfrey Show about gratitude journaling. At that time I was still dealing with a lot of self-esteem issues and struggled with feeling good enough to show up as my authentic self. I was also a people pleaser and would over give my need to feel validated.

Gratitude journaling was the tool that helped me to shift my perspective and move through the negativity that I was feeling in that moment. What I realized is that in life we all have difficulties that we are working through, lessons that we are learning in order to grow, but it is our attitude towards those challenges that will dictate the outcome.

Lessons for Modern Women
The Divine Balance of Strength, Compassion, and Vision

1. *Resilience and Self-Belief*
- Oprah's early struggles remind us as women to rise above challenges and believe in our worth. Know that all the hardships you have endured were supposed to happen to grow your soul on this journey.
- Key Takeaway: Life's hardships can be the foundation of your strength and purpose.

Modern Application:
- When facing challenges and difficulties in life, focus on what you can control and what the universe is trying to teach you about life rather than the obstacles in your midst.
- Set small, achievable goals to build your confidence and develop a growth mindset. Taking small steps each day will get you to your goal.
- Seek out role models or mentors who inspire you to be the best version of yourself.

2. *Authenticity and Connection*
- Oprah's success stems from her ability to be vulnerable and genuinely empathize with her audience.
- Key Takeaway: Authenticity and vulnerability are superpowers. When you show up as your true self, you create deeper connections with people who are on the same vibration as you.

Modern Application:
- Practice active listening and open communication in relationships to foster trust.
- Embrace vulnerability by sharing your experiences with trusted people, allowing them to connect with the real you.
- Build a personal brand that aligns with your true values and beliefs.

3. *Ownership and Leadership*
- By taking ownership of her brand, Oprah demonstrated the importance of controlling one's narrative and value.
- Key Takeaway: True leadership isn't about force; it's about vision, strategy, recognizing your unique gifts, and understanding how to cultivate the gifts and talents of others.

Modern Application:
- Identify areas in your life where you can take more ownership, such as finances, career goals, or setting personal boundaries.
- Develop your leadership skills through courses, workshops, or hands-on experiences.

- Lead by example, using empathy, compassion, and collaboration to inspire those around you.

4. *Service and Purpose*
- Oprah's philanthropy shows that living on purpose means using your influence to uplift others.
- Key Takeaway: Purpose aligns with service. The more you give, the more fulfillment you receive. This is a universal law.

Modern Application:
- Find causes that resonate with your passions and values and volunteer your time.
- Use your skills to mentor or support someone who is navigating challenges you've overcome.
- Each quarter of the year carve out time to reflect on how your work or personal life contributes to the well-being of others.

5. *Spiritual Growth and Alignment*
- Oprah's emphasis on spiritual growth teaches women to prioritize inner peace and clarity. Mind, body, and soul balance is important work that allows you to flourish in all areas of your life.
- Key Takeaway: Align with your higher self to walk confidently in your divine feminine energy.

Modern Application:
- Develop a daily mindfulness practice, such as meditation, journaling, or gratitude exercises.

- Create a personal vision board to focus on your goals and align them with your inner values.
- Dedicate time to explore spiritual or philosophical teachings that resonate with your beliefs.

Oprah Winfrey's life has served as an inspiration for many women. Demonstrating empathy, compassion, vulnerability, and service are powerful feminine tools that can lead to joy, success, and fulfillment. She has shown that by connecting to the global human experience, if your heart is open, you can find a piece of your soul in everyone and that by doing this you tap into an infinite source of wisdom and power that transcends race, skin color, nationality, gender, religion, and political lines.

> *In my journey to collect wisdom, my feminine power, and be a better human being I deeply feel as women we can heal the world.*

We have such a powerful influence on those around us and if we dedicate ourselves to practicing feminine principles and dive deep into our purpose we can collectively release a magical force that brings us together as humans on our home called Earth.

> *Mother Earth is waiting for her daughters to answer the call. How will you respond?*

We are in a very critical place and time as human beings, and I strongly believe that your divine purpose is needed more than ever. Playing small won't cut it anymore.

Radiant Reset Journaling

On the following pages, you'll find journaling prompts.

Each question is designed to reveal an ever-evolving divine potential that is rooted in your divine purpose.

It is my intention to inspire you to believe and celebrate the many ways your divine purpose is needed more than ever.

What drives me? What gifts do I have that I can bring to the table?

_____
_____
_____
_____
_____
_____
_____
_____
_____
_____
_____
_____
_____
_____

AMAZING WOMAN DIVINE LEGACY

What experiences in my life have been painful? How can I alchemize that pain into power?

_____

_____

_____

_____

_____

_____

_____

_____

_____

_____

_____

_____

_____

_____

AMAZING WOMAN DIVINE LEGACY

How can I practice more compassion and empathy for others? Are there any internal biases I have towards people who are different from me that prevent me from finding a piece of myself in them?

_____
_____
_____
_____
_____
_____
_____
_____
_____
_____
_____
_____
_____
_____

AMAZING WOMAN DIVINE LEGACY

Candice Smith Güzelişik

How can I be more intentional about building community with other women?

AMAZING WOMAN DIVINE LEGACY

Who is one woman who reflects qualities and values I'd like to expand in my own life? What are those qualities and values? What are one or more actions I can take now to embody those qualities and values in my own life?

AMAZING WOMAN DIVINE LEGACY

About Candice Smith Güzelişik

Candice Güzelişik is a mother, teacher, multi-passionate entrepreneur, author, dancer, and lover of life. She is founder of *Her Expat Life*, an organization that helps women who live, work, and travel abroad to build community. She is originally from the United States. After going on vacation to Italy with a friend, she made the spontaneous decision to move to Rome. In a matter of weeks after returning to the US, she packed up all her belongings, her autistic daughter, her dogs, and hightailed it to Rome, Italy. She now lives between Malaga, Spain and Istanbul, Turkey where she purchased property and has built an amazing life for herself and her daughter.

For more information about Candice Smith Güzelişik and her work, visit her on social media on LinkedIn: https://www.linkedin.com/in/candicesmithherexpatlife/

Or email her at candicesmith@herexpatlife.com

Dedicated to all the women who are finding the courage to bring about one revelation at a time, line by line, to allow the awakening to begin… the women who know we can uplift and mentor each other… the ones who trust that together we can move each other out of fear and change the perspective that every life is beautiful and impactful.

Ella Nebeker

Chapter 8

Finding Stillness Through Self-Love:
A Most Radiant Quality of Your Divine Nature

Ella Nebeker

"There are times in our lives where a revolution of the soul brings the revelations needed to guide us back to self-love.

A revolution of the soul can look like a crisis: the end of a marriage, the death of a child or partner, or even life-threatening illnesses.

Our soul is calling us to awaken.
And so, it begins one revelation at a time.
Beginning with one act of self-love at a time.
Line upon line, at every age, though the beauty of self-love we begin to rise."
—Ella Nebeker

Can beauty be magnified through self-love?

Self-love is offering the same kindness to ourselves that we offer to a stranger. It is seeing the beauty in every situation and every person. When you love yourself, you glow from the inside out. Whether you are a Maiden, a Mother, or a Monarch, self-love will illuminate your life. It will help you attract your tribe, those who resonate with your dreams, and those who respect and love you for who you are. Everything starts with how you feel about yourself. Start feeling worthy, brilliant, and beautiful. Be willing to receive all that this life has to offer.

Every great teacher has weighed in on self-love. In the New Testament in the book of Mathew, 22:34-40, Jesus tells us to love God with all our hearts and to love our neighbor as ourselves. Buddha teaches that you must love The Self before extending unconditional love. Self-love and compassion are qualities of your divine nature. The Torah teaches us to love our fellow as ourselves. Islam teaches it is imperative to love oneself in order to love others.

We come into this world with love, awe, honesty, excitement for life, and the ability to learn. Gradually we relinquish these through our choices, cultural experiences, and sometimes well-meaning family, friends, and teachers at church or school.

How do we practice self-love when our sense of self is broken and our sense of belonging has been compromised?

Our mothers and grandmothers did the very best they could. Sometimes they were limited in their capacity or circumstance to show us the maternal love that we all need to get started. This can lead to a sense of not belonging and a deep, heartbreaking loneliness. You are not alone, and I promise you that there are other ways to find that maternal love and nurturing that may have eluded you and kept you from learning self-love. By healing ourselves through self-love, we can change things for our children, our children's children, and our mothers and grandmothers. In this healing, we all rise. Our mothers and grandmothers are freed from the burdens that they were unable to define and heal. Our children will rise to be better parents, better human beings, and even better citizens of this world.

Many of us create a False Self as we grow up. Sometimes we lose ourselves in marriage or divorce as young mothers, or perhaps we feel hopeless and without value as we age. The beauty of this awareness is that we can change it. We can find ourselves and love ourselves again. We can begin again. As we implement self-love into our lives, we meet our authentic selves.

The Universe has a way of providing exactly what and who we need to show us the way. Throughout my life, I found role models in women who nurtured themselves and others. As early as elementary school I began identifying them. One of the first women was a classmate's mother. She was lovely, a hard worker, and an amazing horticulturist. Everything she grew was lush, healthy, and bountiful. Her gift for arranging flowers was poetic, but her real gift was how she made me feel about myself. She always had a kind uplifting word and treated me as an equal. Another woman was my high school art teacher. She knew how to care for herself. She was bold, gorgeous, and shared great wisdom. Her best advice to me was, "Get out of 'Dodge' right after graduation." I listened and began a great adventure two thousand miles away from home. My art teacher spent her life being a mothering influence for hundreds, if not thousands, of young girls. Women like these set the example of nurturing in positive ways. They had healthy boundaries and were strong.

> *God has always sent the angels I've needed.*
> *We must open our eyes, ears, hearts,*
> *and minds to see them.*
> *As a child, they showed up as*
> *neighbors, teachers, parents of friends, and in books.*
> *All of them were imperfect, but perfect for me.*

Later as a mother of small children, my vision of anything beyond that was non-existent. You might say I was in the thick of what I had always imagined to be my life purpose. Life has a way of bringing up our fears so we can face them. Suddenly, I was divorced for the second time at forty. I was scared I would end up alone, sitting in a chair for the next forty years just like my grandma did after my grandpa passed on. Her body became molded to the shape of that chair. She quit living and just existed. This image had me scared half to death. One day, out of the blue, a wise friend gave me a precious gift: a black and white photo of a stunning, incandescent woman in her late fifties. This photo became my vision for the future. Having no idea who she was, I simply embraced her as family and hung her in my hall gallery with the faces of my beloved children. Her dynamic, radically honest, all-knowing presence somehow gave me great hope. Over time, she became my silent teacher. It was there in her quiet radiance that I began to recognize myself. I allowed her silence to guide me to become a confident, radiant, inspired woman. She gave me hope for my future. We all need mentors to guide us into every chapter of our lives.

Gradually I stopped fighting growing older and began aging into beauty. I let my hair turn silver and white and grew it long and wild down my back. Wrinkles became the precious evidence that I had lived with courage, labored with might, and laughed with joy. Finally, instead of feeling like a lost cause, I began taking up a cause: my cause. I found authenticity in who I am and embraced our cause of changing the way we think about growing older.

> *Angels show up in many ways to*
> *help us understand that we are loved*
> *and that there is hope for all of us.*
> *Some angels are alive,*
> *some are heavenly,*
> *and some are seeds sown into the fabric of our souls,*
> *left waiting to be awakened.*
> *Let the revelations begin.*

Revelation is the Revolution of the Soul.
There are times in our lives where a revolution of the soul brings the revelations needed to guide us back to self-love. A revolution of the soul can look like a crisis, the end of a marriage, the death of a child or partner, or even life-threatening illnesses. Our soul is calling us to awaken. And so, it begins one revelation at a time. Beginning with one act of self-love at a time. Line upon line, though love we begin to rise.

Ella Nebeker

Revelations of Self-Love #1
The Feeding of One's Spirit Begins with Gratitude

My journey back to loving myself began when I was thirty-four, a divorced mother with six children between the ages of five months and eight years old. I came upon a book that changed my life called *"Simple Abundance: A Daybook of Comfort and Joy,"* by Sarah Ban Breathnach. I will forever be grateful to her. This was my new beginning, my introduction to the power of gratitude, and my new awareness of seeing the beauty that was all around me. My eyes began to open to a brighter present, filled with awe, beauty, and newfound hope for the future. This was my first revelation in a very long time with many more to come. Line upon line, precept upon precept, we learn to love ourselves as God loves us.

The opportunities for self-love are forever unfolding.
It's not one big revelation as much
as it is a series of small revelations
that begin to enlighten and awaken the soul.

It's noticing the red geraniums against the ocher-yellow house that you have driven past hundreds of times. It's the sound of children's laughter as your ears awaken and take notice. It's the feeling of moss under your bare feet as they kiss the earth, grounding you in this magical world. It's the smell of fall leaves, bonfires, and hot apple cider. It's the taste of local honey drizzled on warm, homemade bread. It's that still, small voice that begins to rumble inside you, speaking from your authentic self. That is the revelation that erupts from the revolution of the soul. Self-love is the awakening of all of the senses. Self-love begins with gratitude.

Revelation of Self-Love #2
Comfort Soothes the Soul

Just as a baby needs soothing, so do we. We tend to forget this because life is full of responsibilities, jobs, relationships, and stressful demands. Many of us choose to self-medicate, which is the opposite of self-soothing.

There are better ways.

This is one way I found mine.

My curiosity about cultures, religions, and sacred rituals led me to Feng Shui. I read every book I could get my hands on. I studied with a Master and became a certified Feng Shui consultant. It was a quest to help myself, but then my experience became a way to help others. It was on this journey that I discovered a new way to create vision boards using the BAU GUA, THE CIRCLE OF LIFE. The elements of the earth called to me to balance my life. Part of the course included a personality test. I scored high in the fire, wood, and earth elements. I lived for growth, passion, and expansion, but I was lacking in water and metal energies. Water represents calmness, retrospect, and rebirth. Metal represents strength and discipline.

I began by spending more time with water. We happened to have purchased a fixer-upper with a 1950's kidney-shaped pool. The renovation came to a screeching halt when my second husband decided he no longer wanted to be married. That pool was my saving grace. Cleaning it became my meditation in the early hours before the kids got up. During my divorce, that water helped heal my broken heart. I pulled a cushion next to the edge and laid there listening to the calming sounds of the water lapping back and forth. When fall arrived, I turned up the heater and continued to swim at night after the kids went to sleep. The earth elements have a way of soothing us.

We find ways to self-soothe through self-care, healthy food, music, continued education, movement, and finding joy in this beautiful planet and those we love.

Whether it's hiking, biking, walking on the beach, or putting our feet in the soil while planting our spring gardens, Mother Earth has the power to soothe and heal.

Revelation of Self-Love #3
Becoming the Calm in Life's Storm by Stilling the Noise of the Mind

My introduction to meditation was a Tibetan mantra about letting go and letting God in. I love that mantra. (I still chant it often, especially in the shower).

"Gate, gate, paragate, parasamgate. Bodhi svaha."
Translation:
Gone, gone, gone beyond.
Oh, what an awakening.

Later I learned that many different things can be used as meditation: the simplicity of lighting a candle, the mundane chore of making a bed, the breathtaking beauty of the sunrise, or even the drizzle of rain. Hand washing the dishes is sacred, calming, and real.

One of my favorite fun meditations is to buy a bottle of kid's bubbles for blowing. I'll sit on my balcony, blow bubbles, and observe. Each is unique in size and shape. They dance as the wind carries them away, and I imagine my worries being carried away with them.

Another favorite meditation of mine is being in my garden feeling the breeze and the grass and breathing in the fragrant flowers as if to become one with them. Getting my hands dirty on the earth has always been healing. Nature can be our best meditation. Some Japanese doctors prescribe a forest walk to help still the minds of those suffering from anxiety and depression. Trees can bring such an overwhelming sense of calm to all our senses.

When we take time to breathe in beauty, we experience stillness. It's as though the mind slows down. It helps us be and live in the present moment more often. I have a favorite shop in Salt Lake City called *"Ward and Child Garden Store."* It's my feel-good place. Just walking in the door washes peace over me. I've had the privilege of introducing my clients to this magical place. It is truly a blissful experience. There is a glorious secret garden in the back that is a perfect place to find the peace one longs for in this world.

Meditation calms my soul and replaces jumbled nerves with a connection to self and God. Many things are meditations, including bubbles, gardens, and doing the dishes. As we begin to see beauty in every person, every task, and every situation in our lives, then and only then do we become one with God, ourselves, and each other.

Revelation of The Warrior Goddess #4
It is in our healing that we can lift our families, communities, country, and world.

It's in our healing and self-love that we can conquer fear, that we can put on the armor of God, the armor of who we are, and the confidence to make real change in this challenging world. When we change, we help to facilitate change in others. It is with confidence that we stand in our power and thus help others to do the same. Together we will usher in the new earth. Women and men standing shoulder to shoulder, their feet firmly planted in earth, their hearts filled with love, their minds filled with empathy and acceptance.

Heal Thyself and We Heal the World.
In essence, it is only through a sense of belonging and through a series of profound revelations that we can allow ourselves to fully experience self-love. It begins with gratitude, awareness, and connection. People can inspire us and love us unconditionally, but they cannot give us the love that only we can give ourselves. The late Maya Angelo once said, "*If I am not good to myself, how can I expect anyone else to be good to me?*" It took me a long time to learn to be good to me.

*Self-love is Seeing the Beauty
in Every Person and Every Situation.*

One revelation at a time, line by line, we allow the awakening to begin. Together we can uplift and mentor each other. Together we move each other out of fear and change the perspective that every life is beautiful, and impactful. In this awakening, we begin to rise and help others to do the same. We are all connected just as in nature and in the universe.

Ella Nebeker

Radiant Reset Journaling

On the following pages, you'll find journaling prompts.

Each question is designed to bring you revelations needed to guide you back to self-love.

It is my intention to inspire you to explore ways your soul is calling you to awaken, one revelation at a time.

It begins by embracing the beauty of self-love.

At every age we begin to rise!

What is one expression of thankfulness that nurtures your feeling of connection?

Ella Nebeker

What ignites your senses? In what ways can you perceive this as a journey towards a deeper relationship with self-love?

Ella Nebeker

What is one subject that has always piqued your curiosity, inspiring you to delve deeper and broaden your understanding?

___

Ella Nebeker

What is one self-care practice you've often considered or are curious to try?

Ella Nebeker

What setting or activity brings you a profound sense of peace and tranquility?

Ella Nebeker

About Ella Nebeker

As a lover of beauty and a seeker of truth, Ella Nebeker is changing the way we think about growing old.

As a speaker, teacher and multi-published author she teaches the power of embracing life at every age. She is the creator of *The Art of Age Now*, a movement that inspires women to be their best in every decade of their lives. She is married to the man of her dreams and lives in Salt Lake City, Utah.

She has eight grown children and eleven beautiful grandchildren. Pamela invites you to join her on this courageous journey of aging into the radiant beauty of who we truly are.

For more information about Pamela Nebeker and her work visit: www.pamelanebeker.com

Or follow her on Instagram @Pamelanebeker_the_art_of_age

Radiant Insights

There's a radiance of evolving energy arising.
It's calling us forth and into a new kind of confidence
— a sacred confidence —
a more empowered relationship with
the authentic expression of our gifts and abilities —
a welcoming embrace of our wholeness —
a call to rise in the power of our spiritual purpose.

The Awakening of Divine Grace

Rocio Ortiz Luevano

> "Pray to Mother Mary. She is your Spirit Guide.
> She will help you through all times.
> Also meditate and open yourself to
> Eastern philosophies, Buddhism, yoga.
> Read Thich Nhat Han and Marianne Williamson.
> Reconnect with your femininity."

These words were spoken to me almost 15 years ago but remain vividly palpable in my heart and memory. It was my very first encounter with an Intuitive Healer. That session left me with a sense of peace, purpose, and bold empowerment. I had never felt anything like it. It prepared me to make profound and long-lasting changes in my life and ready to heal a long list of subtle and unspoken traumas including generational trauma, early childhood trauma, trauma experienced through the passing of my beloved husband, and trauma experienced simply by being a woman in the world. The path ahead at the time was not entirely clear, but faith in myself and the future fortified by my spiritual practice was all I needed to forge ahead.

My life started to change very rapidly and take a new shape. Initially traveling through the dark night of the soul. For me, the dark night of the soul was rooted in a very difficult, nearly indescribable experience in my first marriage that created a deep wound and profound trauma… his incarceration, caring for our son, managing the home while maintaining focus for my work, looking after his dying father and heartbroken mother, and eventually, our separation and divorce. Going through a myriad of emotions and feelings. Navigating depression, rage, grief, guilt… I had many sleepless nights doubtful if I would be able to lift myself out of the darkness. I wondered. But I stayed with it.

It was as though I could hear Mother Mary say,
"Am I not here, I Who Am your Mother?"

For the first time in my life, I really connected with Mother Mary, praying the rosary every morning and every night, asking her to guide me and light my path. Gradually the knots became untied, things just started to work themselves out, the darkness started to lift. I felt more hopeful. The Blessed Mother would remain ever protective and loving of me.

My desire and motivation for change was strong. A new me wanted to be birthed through this transformation. There was a shedding of the old as the new came forth. It was a spiritual depression which was giving way for a new life. A time of deep spiritual work, introspection, and healing.

Whenever I chanted So Purkh I really felt the difference.
The energy became much lighter, the heaviness lifted.
I was filled with compassion, forgiveness, and love.

Praying So Purkh created major shifts in my life. Shifts and changes began integrating so quickly that my life took on new shapes and forms. I experienced healing of relationships, meeting like-minded people, financial stability, feeling hopeful and positive about the future. It was exciting and compelling for me, and it gave me more energy to stay with my spiritual practice. I was in awe of how quickly change took shape and it gave me the momentum to stay true to my spiritual practice.

*The image that so often comes to mind is
Our Lady of Guadalupe,
Tonantzin, Mother Mary
as she is known throughout the world.*

*She embodies and represents the sacred feminine
and her great capacity for love, forgiveness,
openness, and compassion.*

*She reminds us that we all carry the essence of divinity
and as such we all have the capacity to
transform as well as heal all past, present,
and future wounds and traumas of one's heart.*

*She has become the source,
the reason and inspiration for my sacred power.
I also know and trust
that she has been with me throughout
my entire life supporting me every step of the way.
Guiding and lifting me through the joy
and through the pain.
She will remain ever present.*

But nothing could have prepared me for this… the passing of my beloved.

On January 24, 2022, my beloved Husband Alex Luevano passed away. Losing him crushed my soul to pieces. Initially I felt like I was out of my body, disconnected, I felt rage, frustration, confusion, why us, why me? The pain was excruciating… feelings of abandonment, sadness, depletion, and numbness surfaced. There were moments when I even contemplated joining him. But instead, I wrote about and reflected on our time together… it gave me solace.

Before I met my husband, I wrote a list of attributes I was seeking in a companion. I knew the universe was listening, so I was very specific in my request. Whoever was to show up in my life needed to be the following:

*Confident. Self-assured. Gracious. Compassionate. Kind.
Sensitive to the human spirit. Funny. Forgiving.
Humble and someone who loved his mother and family.
Someone who loved children.
Someone who enjoyed the outdoors and traveling.
Someone who made me laugh and allowed me to be me.*

The man who showed up was the love and soul of my life. Although our time together was brief, he made me incredibly happy. I was heartbroken by his loss yet eternally grateful to have loved such an incredible man.

Today I have come to realize that our life experiences, even those of great trauma, pain and grief can carry the greatest gifts of transformation, expansion, and wisdom.

I feel when we pause, bless, and have gratitude for all our experiences, it liberates and propels us forward towards a deep healing. Allowing us to return to the simplicity of wholeness.

Now more than ever I feel compelled and inspired to help other women find their own healing, find their own feminine gifts… to emerge and awaken through Divine Grace… to reveal their true, powerful and authentic selves.

About Rocio Ortiz Luevano

Rocio Ortiz Luevano is a Licensed Clinical Social Worker, Infant-Family and Early Childhood Mental Health Specialist, Reiki Practitioner, first generation Mexican-American and best-selling author.

Through neuroscience, spirituality and her personal story, Rocio encourages women to find their own strength and potential for inner healing. It is also through their own healing that they can powerfully create healing for their children and future generations.

For over twenty years, Rocio has served and supported vulnerable mothers and very young children in the Los Angeles area who have experienced and been affected by trauma or adversity. Her aim has been to foster emotional healing and empowerment, as well as ending generational trauma for mothers and babies. Her hope is to help them unearth their innate capacity for emotional healing as well as to help them discover healing through a personal spiritual practice.

Rocio stands for non-violent parenting, protection of children from trauma and the uncompromised respect for women. Her multitude of skills as a Clinician and Teacher including spiritually mindedness, Neuroscience informed, Trauma-informed and Reiki Healer, allows her to help people from a psycho-educational, neuroscientific and spiritual perspective.

Her vision is to help women who have experienced trauma or challenging situations to emerge, transform and embrace their freedom and simultaneously heal, protect and create resilience for their children.

For more information about Rocio Ortiz Luevano visit: www.chiopsw@gmail.com

Or, on Instagram at @chiopsw

Awakening the Power of Your Spiritual Path

Niloo Golshan

There comes a time when we must let go of old beliefs, discard the masks that no longer align with our true selves. These beliefs, doubts, and fears — they whisper constantly in our minds, pretending to keep us safe. But in truth, they anchor us to past habits and patterns that no longer serve our highest good.

In 1978, at the age of 13, riots broke out in Tehran, and my parents, seeking safety, planned what was meant to be a brief escape to Israel.

Months later, the heart of Israel, a realization dawned that we would never return to Iran. And my world shifted. The upheaval started in Tehran, had transformed a supposed short vacation into a permanent exile. As weeks turned into months, the whispers of adults around me painted a grimmer picture. Iran was on the brink of a revolution; it was no longer safe to return. That was the moment my childhood innocence was shattered, and I was suddenly thrust into an abyss of uncertainty, grappling with the loss of my home, my friends, and all that was familiar.

After nine months in Israel, my family's path took us to New York and, eventually, to Los Angeles. Each relocation was a fresh start, a new battle against the tide of instability. In New York, I was a foreigner in a sea of unfamiliar faces, where my homeland was known only for its war-torn image, not for the rich culture and kindness that defined the true Iran.

Yet in these times of change, and throughout my life, I found unexpected anchors — "earth angels" in the form of friends who appeared when I needed them most, offering solace and connection. They stood as a testament to the divine's presence in my life, reassuring me that even as I navigated the loss of my homeland, I was still connected to something greater — a universal tapestry of human connection and resilience.

When I arrived in Los Angeles, I entered a world that was both familiar and alien. The city housed a large Persian community, many of whom, like my family, were refugees. Each person carried their own narrative of escape and loss, a mosaic of stories echoing my own.

Yet, amid this shared backdrop, I found an unexpected disconnect. Despite being surrounded by those with similar origins, I felt an inexplicable distance, a gap between them and me.

As I navigated this path, I found myself struggling with my identity, searching answers to *"Who am I? What am I doing here? Where am I going?"* These questions urged me to find a connection and became an integral part of my journey.

*The driving force to remain true to my spiritual path
was fueled by a deeper, more compelling motivation
— my two young daughters.
The love for my daughters became my beacon,
guiding me through uncertainty.*

The only consistency in my life has been a devotion to spiritual practice, a connection to the divine, and my faith in the universe.

I vividly recall one life changing moment. While soaking in the warm and embracing waters of a Jacuzzi, a soft, gentle voice spoke to me:

*"Dear Child, how can I continue guiding you
if you ignore my messages?"*

Later, I realized it was the voice of the Divine Feminine guiding me. And I knew that from that day on, in ordert o evolve on my spiritual path, I must listen to the inner voice of the Divine Feminine.

*I made a profound promise:
to heed and act upon all divine guidance, not just
the convenient parts. This vow steered me towards
deepening my embrace of the Divine Feminine.*

Previously, my perception was filtered, tuning out anything that might unsettle my seemingly perfect life. To the outside world, I appeared to have everything. Inwardly, however, I was merely existing in a numb state of autopilot.

*I began to understand that listening
to the divine voice meant embracing change,
even if it meant stepping into the unknown.
It was about breaking free from the autopilot mode
that had kept me safe but unfulfilled.
I must venture into the uncharted territories
of self-discovery and truth.*

This realization sparked a devotion to reinvent myself, despite not knowing where to start or how to proceed. I found myself at a crossroads, facing the daunting task of dismantling the life I knew to uncover the authentic "me" that had been buried under years of conformity and expectation. This process of awakening was not just about physical healing; it was something more. It was a spiritual awakening.

*It was like undergoing a metamorphosis, a deep and
personal change, and I feel it's important to
convey this to you as you walk your own path.*

I've grappled with false voices in my mind — voices of doubt, fear, and outdated beliefs — all masquerading as protectors keeping me "safe." Yet, I realized that these false voices were chains holding me back, preventing me from surrendering to my highest self and moving forward in life.

*This process was not gentle or easy. It demanded that I sit
with myself, confront, and embrace every emotion that
surfaced, without judgment or the urge to control.*

I was guided to dive deep into the dark side of the Divine Feminine to see my pain. Feel it fully, giving myself permission to let these emotions move through me. By facing and freeing emotions that had been trapped within me for so long, they transformed and became lessons, purposes, guides to my next steps.

This liberation was crucial. It meant no longer being stuck in a loop of repeating the same old patterns. I was creating a new space within myself, a space where I could cultivate thoughts and beliefs that were authentic and spoke truth.

This encounter with the dark side of the Divine Feminine opened my eyes to the profound wounding of the divine feminine within my own culture, particularly as a woman from the Middle East.

I realized that the promise of healing wasn't just for me; it extended to my daughters as well, offering a chance to break the cycle of generational wounds and prevent their transmission to future generations.

There's a saying that resonates deeply with me:
'when one woman heals herself,
she also heals seven generations before and after her.'

I committed to my healing journey, a path that involved not only personal introspection but also a broader quest to restore the generational and ancestral traumas ingrained in my family's bloodline.

When we awaken the Sacred Divine Feminine energy, we become present, empathetic, and deeply connected to others. We reawaken qualities of intuition, nurturing, creativity, emotional intelligence, and compassion.

My journey is a testament to the transformative power of the Divine Feminine. It's about finding your truth, stepping into the unknown, and surrendering to her inner whisper.

As I share my words with you, I hope to convey that this journey of transformation is deeply personal yet universally relevant. It's about stepping boldly into a future where we live as our most authentic selves. This path I've walked is not just my story — it's a testament to the power and the courage to embrace one's true self.

I'm here to remind you, beloved sister, that you too, are Divine. You, too, are the Goddess merging with the Divine Feminine. I am here to help you remember your authenticity, your truth, your beauty, your love, your strength, your power, your grace, and all that you may have forgotten. As I did.

Sharing my experiences with you here, I have done so with an open heart. I hope that in reading my journey, you find the strength to confront your own fears, to embrace your own journey of self-discovery, and to recognize that in the tapestry of life, every thread, every color, every shade is vital to the complete picture.

Niloo Golshan

And as we, as women, awaken the power of our unique and individual spiritual path, it is my prayer that we remember our sense of connection and belonging… always celebrating the resilient women who have shaped our lives, our female lineage, our grandmothers, our sisters, our daughters. May we know our strength, remember our power, and radiantly walk our Divine Legacy together.

About Niloo Golshan

Teacher, Mentor, Alchemist, and Sensory Transformation Facilitator

Niloo is a devoted Spiritual guide with over four decades of experience on a journey of self-realization and inner transformation. With a rare blend of empathy, a delightful sense of humor, and a talent for evoking joy, she creates spaces that awaken all five senses, inspiring a holistic approach to a healthy lifestyle. Niloo is a proud mother of 2 wise and well-rounded beautiful daughters.

Drawing from her personal journey through unimaginable hardships as a refugee, navigating challenging chronic health conditions, and a turbulent marriage, Niloo has undergone profound transformations in health, wealth, and personal relationships, shaping her into a compassionate and insightful mentor.

Since 2005, Niloo has been dedicated to teaching and guiding women inward, helping them rediscover their essence, truth, purpose, and inherent feminine strength. Through her commitment to creating beautiful and sacred rituals and spaces, she provides a nurturing environment where transformation can take place. Utilizing a wealth of experience in teaching Kundalini yoga and meditation, breathwork, Restorative yoga, women's healing circles, dance and movement, Bhakti yoga, and leading Kirtans, Niloo serves as a skilled healing practitioner, harnessing the power of the senses.

Niloo also offers compassionate guidance as a Death Doula supporting individuals and their loved ones through life's end, providing assistance in this deeply meaningful phase.

Her spiritual journey includes transformative pilgrimages to India and initiations into advanced Kriya meditations, immersion in the Sacred Geometry mystery school in Bali, as well as mystical initiations in the ancient goddess temples of Egypt.

With this rich tapestry of knowledge, wisdom and hands-on experience, Niloo is passionately committed to leading and supporting women on their paths of personal evolution and self-exploration. Niloo's dedication to the care of self and others inspires women to courageously reconnect with their body and spirit, re-claiming their power to speak up, to stand up for themselves, to show up, and to share their unique gifts with the world.

For more information about Niloo Golshan and her work visit: www.niloogolshan.com

Write to her at: contact@niloogolshan.com

My Legacy

Carol Patricia Koppelman

The Culmination of my Life Experiences and a Homage to my Ancestral Heritage

We try on different identities throughout our lives, often in response to social norms or what we perceive to be social norms. I look back at my 26-year-old self. I had a perfect hourglass figure, perfect skin, long, auburn hair. I had a career in business administration and participated in a local theater group. My persona was "happy party girl," dancing and partying every night. But I was socially anxious and because of that and the crowd I ran with, I drank too much. My romances, when not shallow, were devastatingly painful experiences with equally vapid, artistic, and often broke men.

In my early 30's, I returned to college to finish my bachelor's degree. I took on the identity of "mature student" — all business, which included the usual props — spectacles that I didn't need, the serious brow. I fit in more with the professors than the students, and eventually my facade was blown. My first newspaper job out of college, I was sniffing out and exposing corruption, but it was just another façade. I was a scared newbie, and although several articles were picked up by the AP, the pay sucked, and I soon left for the corporate sector.

From my mid 30's through early 60's, I played the Fortune 500 corporate game. I dressed to the nines; I played the man's game because it was a man's world. I encountered sexual harassment when you had no recourse, sophistry that would make my skin crawl, and marched to the beat of the corporate cult song. I muffled my intuition.

In my early 60's, I retired from corporate life and have never been freer. I've spent several years healing, with the help of several modalities, a dysregulated nervous system. I realized that some of my dysregulation was a result of muffling my authentic voice for years in pursuit of what the world defined as success. This release has allowed my intuition, heart, soul, mind, and gut to align. It's also given me time to reflect on the rich influence of my ancestors.

My maternal grandmother was a suffragette, my paternal Italian-born great-grandmother was a gypsy, my mother (whose descendants are from Ireland) has always a had sixth sense. I now honor my heritage and realize that when I "know" something, I need to listen, as this is a gift from God that He has given my ancestral lineage.

Although I would love my youthful figure, looks, and vigor back, I would not trade it for any of my 68-year-old wisdom, contentment, and freedom. My identity is no longer dependent on outward validation; it is a beautiful blend of fusion with God, with self-acceptance, and with a commitment to a joy path.

It is time to honor our ancestral heritage, rich with strong, vibrant women with strong intuitive sense. Our legacy is filled with generations of women who share inherent gifts from the Divine.

Carol Patricia Koppelman

*Consider how your ancestors
are calling you to incorporate the best of
their legacy into your own ever-evolving purpose.*

Here is a practice to support you in tapping into your divine legacy:

PRACTICE
What have you learned from your ancestral lineage and living elders?

- Make a list of their accomplishments and the effect on your life.

- Make a list of what you honor and what you'd like to heal for generations past, present, and future, so that the legacy, from this point forward, is clear of ancestral pain and suffering.

- In prayerful meditation, surrendering to God's Divine direction, honor your ancestors from whom your gifts are borne by thanking them and your living elders for their contribution to the world. Tell them that you will continue their work and pass on this legacy to future generations. Ask God to heal ancestral pain and suffering, so that you and future generations will continue their legacy with a clear heart, mind, and spirit.

- After this exercise, make a list of how you feel you can best represent your rich ancestral legacy in the world today.

About Carol Patricia Koppelman

Carol Patricia Koppelman is the bestselling author of *Do the Necessary, Let the Rest Go to Hell*. Additionally, she is a featured contributor to multiple International Bestsellers.

As a Branch Director for Park Lane Jewelry, Carol styles women with beautiful jewelry, emphasizing their intrinsic beauty.

Her website: parklanejewelry.com/rep/carolkoppelman

She is also CEO of CPK Solutions, LLC, an Arizona-based business. Her website is cpksolutions.com.

Our Presence

Conni Ponturo

*"Our presence is amplified as we learn
ways to honor our body, mind, and heart."*

*One of the most important questions
we can ask ourselves is:
How can I embody the elegance
of being present in my own power?*

Presence is power. It's an energetic quality that infuses our creativity to manifest the wealth of the moment and the vision of our future. When we aren't present it is impossible to see our value — to feel our worth. Essentially, denying ourselves the elegance of being present to our power is when we are unable to see our true strengths, unable to honor the gifts we are here to share.

*To embody our presence isn't always easy in a world
that has taught us to focus outward rather than inward.
But, with new focus, we can retrain ourselves to
embrace our presence from the inside out
— in our body, our mind, and our heart.*

Here are three ways to begin to embody your presence by engaging the body, the mind, and the heart:

In My Body: I started to anchor in the idea of ALLOWING my worth. This is not an easy feeling to anchor in. There is so much fear that comes up with the word "worth." Most of us at one time or another has felt unworthy. The question we ask most is "*Who am I to feel worthy?*" Thoughts and feelings erupted inside me, and I didn't like it, and the way it made me feel. I didn't want to sift and sort through the muck of self-doubts that I had, it was easier to keep it down and hidden. I kept coming back to "*Why don't I value myself?*" I began to practice more self-love and self-care. I practiced kindness with myself, and I began to treat myself as worthy, valuable, and deserving. I treated exercise as a gift to myself, which allowed me to connect with my body, but also, it allowed me to connect on a deeper level with my soul.

In My Mind: I began to practice the intentional use of my words. I became conscious of what I was saying and what the words communicated. I devoted myself to practice Yoga Nidra meditation and breathwork daily, which took me out of the overthinking monkey mind and dropped me back into my heart. It allowed me to take a step back and distance myself from unworthy thoughts, and it allowed me to be present in the moment. Sometimes circumstances are not easy. They can be stressful and hurtful, but I had to allow the emotions to flow through me, instead of holding on so tightly. If I wanted to have a different, more expanded life, I had to be present in the words I used, and I had to begin to use better, more abundant words, on a more consistent basis. I had to believe that I was worthy of all the fantastic opportunities entering my life. But I had to do more than that, I had to believe in my new vision for my life.

In My Heart: I realized how little time I was giving my heart. Dropping into my intuition I was shown that I was moving much too fast to even hear the whispers. Then, a crazy thing happened, I started feeling a tingling in the back of my neck. I made sure that I went to the doctor and checked it out to make sure nothing was wrong, but I began to feel like it was telling me something. Have heard the phrase, *He's a pain in the neck?* I began to feel the tingle in my neck was trying to tell me something important. Not that I had a brain tumor or something was wrong, but rather something was right, and I needed to listen. I had to start loving myself and it was time to integrate my new truths throughout both my inner and my outer life. I had to allow my inner-longings and desires to become actions. I had to re-access my worthiness and let myself experience more of life. I could no longer deny my desires. I began to step into the forefront of my life and show up in the world: for myself, for others, for my work, and my life.

> *Presence is your ability to experience*
> *the fullness in each moment.*

Presence — being aware and connected in the moment — standing perfectly still, aware and content to be right where you are. Not striving to look too far ahead or gazing behind but standing still — that's where the real wealth of presence shows itself.

What does it mean to be present?

1. It means you are awake in your life.

2. You are fully aware and connected to your body and the environment around you.
3. You notice what's around you and are open to opportunities.
4. You are in the truth of your body.
5. You are not looking behind or ahead.
6. You allow yourself to stop and stand still.
7. You immerse yourself in a sense of calm and joy that only a state of presence can bring.

Do you feel present in your life?

Feet fully planted on the ground in every moment?

Or do you feel like you are just going through the motions of life, everything passing you by, and suddenly, you pick your head up, and months or years have gone by?

The truth is the fullness of your life is calling to you right now.

It is speaking to you through moment-by-moment experiences.

It is calling to you through the creative longings of your heart.

It's whispering and reminding you of the elegance of being present to your power.

How will you allow this power to define your Divine Legacy?

About Conni Ponturo

*"Living a pain-free, ageless life
is only possible when we understand
the power of creating a harmonious connection with
our mindset, emotions, and physical bodies."*

Conni Ponturo is a leading authority in the field of pain-free living, which includes the power of creating a harmonious connection of mindset, emotions, and body. Respected for her unique approach to Transformational Movement that merges Pilates, meditation, breathwork, and mindset, Conni Ponturo teaches her clients how to flourish at every stage and age.

Her latest book "Listen Watch What You Say, Your Body is Listening" is a bestseller on Amazon. She travels the world teaching and speaking about easy-to-do techniques that allow you to connect with your body in a deep and lasting way.

Her expertise in rehabilitative training makes her highly sought after by the medical community for her ability to create a safe environment for recovery from hip replacements, spinal fusions, knee replacements, and other serious injuries. Conni holds multiple certifications from the *Pilates Method Alliance, Balanced Body*, and *Physical Mind Institute*. She is a certified Breast Cancer Exercise Specialist with *The Pink Ribbon Program*.

Conni Ponturo knows that the answer to pain-free living is within us.

She says, "When we truly investigate the connection between our thoughts, beliefs, and lifestyle patterns, we find that we can gain deeper insights into optimizing our freedom to move and live pain-free."

To learn more about Conni Ponturo and her work visit: https://absolutelygrounded.com

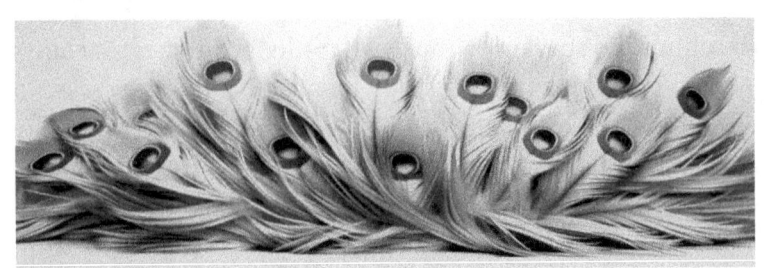

Amazing Woman,
when we stand next to another
and speak our truth something takes place…
others gain access to sacred sight…
others see a reflection of what it looks like
to stay true to our heart, the esteem of our soul.

A shift takes place… a radiant reset ignites…
a new realm of confidence emerges.

We lift one another…
we link arms and rise
in the unbridled expression of our
Spiritual Purpose.

We rise in our Divine Legacy.

The dawn of a radiant reset is upon us.

It's being led by women just like you — the woman who knows it is time to claim her sacred confidence and rise in her spiritual purpose.

CLAIM YOUR SACRED CONFIDENCE. RISE IN YOUR SPIRITUAL PURPOSE.

Write Your RADIANT RESET Statement

A Radiant Reset Statement is a powerful proclamation. It's a declaration of intention… a sacred agreement entered into with yourself, an agreement that serves to align with a new narrative of spiritual purpose — unveiling an inner strength to shift away from a culture steeped in fitting in, leaning in, performing, conforming and settling for status quo — freeing yourself from the obstruction of ideas about how you 'should' act, behave, contribute, accomplish, and realize your divine potentials.

This statement is not about setting goals but rather about cultivating a radiant mindset and the sacred confidence necessary to pursue the highest vision of your future. In this way it can be seen as a promise to hold yourself accountable… a devotion to answer the call of the woman you are meant to be.

The strong, the brave, and fearless. Yes, we notice them. Admire them. Maybe even long to be like them. But it's the vulnerable ones who capture our heart and captivate our Soul. Those are the ones who move and inspire us. Those are the ones we remember.

Write Your Radiant Reset Statement

As you prepare to write a RADIANT RESET STATEMENT, pause to create a sacred space for self-reflection. Use this quiet time to consider your past successes and challenges. Reflect upon where you are now, and the myriads of ways your future self is calling to you.

Remember, a Radiant Reset isn't about 'fixing' something you've judged as lacking. Rather, a Radiant Reset is about claiming sacred confidence. This is seen as the expression of your giftedness and the callings of your sacred work. That's it. That's sacred confidence. No judgment. Simply, an honoring of the path of spiritual purpose that has brought you to this moment now.

The following provides you with a 4-step practice for claiming the sacred confidence to create your own Radiant Reset.

Pause. Breathe. Center yourself.
And then when you feel ready, begin.

Step 1: Meet the Woman You Are Becoming

Imagine your future self. How are you thriving? What abilities are you sharing? Where are you living? What are you doing? What moves you to do it? And, most importantly, how do you feel?

How will you define the prosperity of your future?

Amazing Woman Divine Legacy

Step 2: Speak Your Vision Aloud.

Select words infused with the energy and qualities that best describe your ideal future. With every word allow yourself to feel as though it has already been realized.

What words best describe how you feel as you speak power into the vision of your future? Write those words in the space below. Then reflect on each word. What do they communicate to you? How do the words inform the direction of your future?

_____
_____
_____
_____
_____
_____
_____
_____
_____
_____

Amazing Woman Divine Legacy

Step 3: Define Your Radiant Reset

Determine what resources, skills, or support you are calling in as you step into your future. Are there new rituals, routines, and habits you wish to adopt? Do you wish to study a new expertise or expand upon an ability? How will you magnify a new alignment with the radiance of your future?

_____
_____
_____
_____
_____
_____
_____
_____
_____
_____
_____
_____
_____

Amazing Woman Divine Legacy

Step 4: Move Forward

What is the one action you will take first? An action can be big… like embracing a new career direction, studying a new skill, or expanding upon an ability. Or the action can be to define a collection of small steps. What's important here that you enter into a Sacred Agreement with yourself to move forward in aligned action.

_____

_____

_____

_____

_____

_____

_____

_____

_____

_____

_____

_____

_____

_____

Amazing Woman Divine Legacy

As you begin to move forward, pause to review your progress. Make necessary adjustments as required. And when necessary define a new RADIANT RESET that will support you as you continue to claim your sacred confidence and rise in your spiritual purpose.

Here are a few affirmations to consider when writing your RADIANT RESET Statement:

- I allow and accept positive opportunities.
- I elevate my worth and honor my worthiness.
- I amplify my authentic voice and easily speak my truth.
- I practice receptivity and allow greater creative ease.
- I trust and know I am here to make a difference.
- I rise in sacred confidence and allow it to guide me.
- I pause and align with the radiance of my soul.
- I expand a richness of awareness in every experience.
- I easily move forward through aligned actions that lead me to my most desired future.

And here are a few feminine frequencies to support you to easily anchor your spiritual purpose. You may wish to consider using one or more of these energetic qualities when writing your statement.

- Connectedness. Wholeheartedness.
- Humility, listening, and learning from others.
- Sincerity: a willingness to speak openly and honestly.
- Patience: a recognition that some shifts emerge slowly.
- Empathy: a sensitivity that promotes understanding.
- Trustworthiness: the strength that inspires confidence.

- Openness, receptivity.
- Flexibility, adapt when circumstances require.
- Vulnerability, bold courage, trust in the unknown.
- Meaning, a sense of purpose.
- Eloquent communication: express your needs clearly and your perspective thoughtfully.
- Being dependable, being impeccable with your word.
- Collaboration, flexibility, and cooperation.

WE BELIEVE THE CREATIVITY OF WOMEN CAN AND WILL TRANSFORM THE WORLD!

Amazing Woman Nation is dedicated to evolving the culture of women's success. Founded by Marsh Engle, the movement is dedicated to elevating every woman's sense of purpose and creativity by curating a collection of educational programs, published books, engaging events, and social impact campaigns positioned to move millions.

Since 2001 AMAZING WOMAN books, training programs, podcasts, and events have been recognized for their unparalleled capacity to move women to develop herself as an entrepreneurial leader, launch mission-driven businesses, and create greater impact in the world.

The AMAZING WOMAN NATION philanthropic initiative joins women in a collective intention to create a more empowered future for the next generation of amazing women. Together we aspire to create a world that fully harnesses the power of women to create lasting and positive change in their own lives, in their communities, and in the world.

Philanthropic contributions have supported leading organizations, including YWCA, DARE (Drug Abuse Resistance Education), RAINN (Rape, Abuse, Incest National Network), National Center for Missing & Exploited Children, CAREorg, YWCA (Eliminating Racism. Empowering Women), Dress for Success (Empowering women to achieve economic independence) and Safe Passage.

If you would like to learn more about THE AMAZING WOMAN NATION podcasts, courses, and events visit: www.AmazingWomanNation.com

Join us on FACEBOOK
https://www.facebook.com/
AMAZINGWOMANNATION/

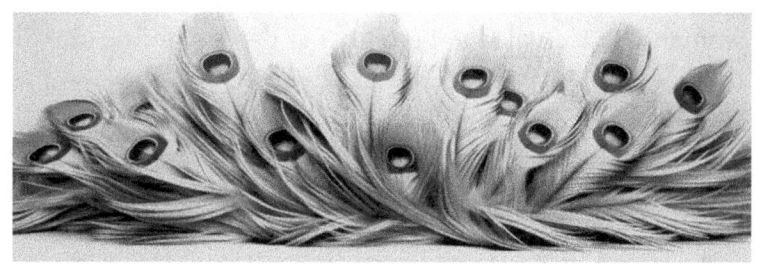

Acknowledgments

Thank you to every woman who believes in the vision of this book. Your sheer commitment to bring your energy, inspiration, words and wisdom to the page moves me to continuously reach higher.

Thank you to my mother and my grandmother for urging me forward in the *search for the amazing woman* leading to my life's work.

Always and forever, love goes to my two sons — Ja and Jon — to my beautiful daughters-in-law, Czerny and Hanae. And to my two grandsons, Jacky and Rio.

Thank you to the thousands of women who have attended *Amazing Woman Live events,* purchased AMAZING WOMAN books and have taken part in AMAZING WOMAN programs — from Maui to Montreal, Los Angeles to Toronto — your commitment to become the amazing woman you are called to become is at the very foundation of the AMAZING WOMAN MOVEMENT.

To the hundreds of clients, past and present, whose purpose and vision are steeped in the wealth of feminine prosperity. It has been my sincere privilege to support you in some way to embrace your most worthy mission.

To my readers and friends who connect with me on my Facebook pages, INSTAGRAM, and LinkedIn. Thank you for the continuous words of encouragement or for simply stopping by to say hello. I love our connection.

I hold great respect for the countless thought leaders and authors, who continue to stir my curiosity, broaden my perspective, and deepen my spiritual connection. Thank you.

To my valued spiritual mentors, colleagues, business consultants, mastermind partners, publisher, and agents… you are forever valued and appreciated.

And, to my cherished friends, thank you for bringing so much inspiration, love, and sheer joy into my life. Your stream of encouragement never fails to move me. And your friendship touches my heart beyond words.

About Marsh Engle

Marsh Engle is devoted to evolving the culture of women's success. Her multi-decade work trailblazes practices that lead women to find and flourish in the richness of their spiritual purpose, reclaiming their voices, and acting upon their highest potentials. Creator of the bestselling AMAZING WOMAN co-authored book series and founder of THE AMAZING WOMAN NATION, her training programs and events are recognized for their unparalleled capacity to move women to define, communicate and realize the radiant wealth of feminine leadership.

In 2016, Marsh served as an elected delegate to THE UNITED STATE OF WOMEN, an acclaimed leadership program led by First Lady Michelle Obama. She's received awards from the Congress of the United States and the City of Los Angeles for her work to elevate women's entrepreneurial leadership. Marsh has shared the stage with bestselling authors including don Miguel Ruiz and Marianne Williamson and acclaimed Journalists Maria Shriver.

Since 1999 her philanthropic contributions have supported leading cause-driven organizations including, DARE (Drug Abuse Resistance Education), RAINN (Rape, Abuse, Incest National Network), Susan G. Komen Breast Cancer Foundation, National Center for Missing & Exploited Children, CARE, YWCA (Eliminating Racism. Empowering Women), Dress for Success (Empowering women to achieve economic independence) and Safe Passage.

For more information about Marsh Engle visit:
www.MarshEngle.com

Connect with Marsh on Facebook:
https://www.facebook.com/marsh.engle/
https://www.facebook.com/OFFICIALMarshEngle/

Connect with Marsh on LinkedIn:
https://www.linkedin.com/in/marshengle

Connect with Marsh on Instagram:
https://www.instagram.com/marshengle/

You are invited to take part in a global community
designed to define a new narrative of sacred
confidence, amplify our giftedness,
and rise in our spiritual purpose.

More Amazing Woman Bestselling Books

https://amzn.to/47SmMzP   https://amzn.to/494HFsz   https://amzn.to/3HxlQpL

Each book in the series of Amazing Woman co-authored books is designed to magnify your giftedness and communicate in ways that amplify your true expression, give deeper self-awareness, and bring significance to your spiritual purpose.

https://geni.us/divinelegacy

For more information about the Amazing Woman co-authored book series visit: www.AmazingWomanNation.com

www.ingramcontent.com/pod-product-compliance
Lightning Source LLC
LaVergne TN
LVHW020925090426
835512LV00020B/3206